RKO CLASSIC SCREENPLAYS

The Mad Miss Manton

Directed by: Leigh Jason
Screenplay by: Philip G. Epstein

An Andrew Velez Book

FREDERICK UNGAR PUBLISHING CO.
New York

Published by arrangement with RKO General, Inc.

PUBLISHER'S NOTE:

This is the complete final screenplay for the RKO film.
The movie as released may differ from the screenplay
in some respects.

Printed in Great Britain
by Biddles of Guildford

ISBN 0-8044-6313-1

INTRODUCTION

A staple figure in scores of films in the 1920s and 30s, the heiress was a leading character who most often was an object of contempt, ridicule, and outright hostility. One of the most successful films of the 30s was the multi-Oscar winning *It Happened One Night* (1934). Its image of a saucy, flighty, and not unsympathetic heiress (played by Claudette Colbert), spawned a whole new flock of celluloid sisters who fled mansions, jilted bridegrooms at the altar, and generally carried on with virtually total disregard for the existence of breadlines, unemployment, and a world headed towards the abyss of another world war.

In the same year as *It Happened One Night*, M-G-M released *The Thin Man*, a mystery both exciting and witty that had William Powell and Myrna Loy exchanging barbs and double entendres.

In 1938, RKO's contribution to the "heiress genre" had Katharine Hepburn as the maddest of them all in *Bringing Up Baby*. Now regarded as a classic, it was perhaps the ultimate "screwball comedy." It was roundly roasted by the critics at the time and flopped at the box office. In the same year the studio released *The Mad Miss Manton*, pairing Barbara Stanwyck and Henry Fonda. Directed by Leigh Jason and scripted by Philip G. Epstein, (based on a story by Wilson Collison), *Manton* had a madcap and impudent heiress as the pivotal figure in a sex-comedy mystery.

Stanwyck is walking her dog at three o'clock in the morning while wearing an incongruous outfit from a costume ball. She happens upon a murder victim in a deserted mansion and calls the police. By the time they turn up, the body has disappeared and it is assumed Melsa Manton is simply up to another of her headline-grabbing stunts. She rounds up a bevy of her silver-foxed girlfriends. Her chums are as concerned about boyfriends, losing weight, parties, and gossiping as they are about finding the body, the murderer, and staying out of his path. Evening dresses seem to be the standard mode of dress. On the sidelines as a wry observer is Stanwyck's maid Hilda, played by Hattie McDaniel in one of her ever-splendid turns, ("You white folks don' know what's good for you-all.").

Henry Fonda, who was teamed again with Stanwyck in Preston Sturges's comedy, *The Lady Eve* (1942), is a newspaper editor who writes an editorial condemning Miss Manton's irresponsible behavior. (As any faithful moviegoer knows, this denotes an inevitable coupling made in cinema heaven.)

The heiress-movie mill continued to churn out such items as *The Cowboy and the Lady* (1938), *Café Society* (1939) and *Lucky Night* (1939). Even Lucille Ball turned up in a "B" version of the role in her pre-"Lucy" days, in *Next Time I Marry* (1938).

As the decade neared an end, television was still in the experimental stage. The use of color in films was advancing technically and gaining in popularity with the public. *You Can't Take It With You* won the Oscar as Best Picture of the Year in 1938 as well as a second gold statue from the Academy for its director, Frank Capra.

At RKO, the studio terminated Katharine Hepburn's contract after she refused the lead in *Mother Carey's Chickens*, believing her career to be over. *Mother Carey*, along with *The Saint in New York*, *Sky Giant*, and *Condemned Women* were RKO's biggest money earners of the year.

Soon heiresses would disappear from the screen, to be replaced by ordinary women in tales of men going off to war. The extravagant hair-dos and gowns of Melsa Manton and her shrieking friends would give way to hair held carefully in place by nets (to avoid being caught in factory machinery!) and slacks and blouses. Time passed, and Miss Manton made way for Mrs. Miniver.

Andrew Velez

CAST:

Melsa Manton	Barbara Stanwyck
Peter Ames	Henry Fonda
Lieutenant Brent	Sam Levene
Helen Frayne	Frances Mercer
Edward Norris	Stanley Ridges
Pat James	Whitney Bourne
Kit Beverly	Vicki Lester
Lee Wilson	Ann Evers
Dora Fenton	Catherine O'Quinn
Myra Frost	Linda Terry
Jane	Eleanor Hansen
Hilda	Hattie McDaniels
Sullivan	James Burke
Bat Regan	Paul Guilfoyle
Frances Glosk	Penny Singleton
Sheila Lane	Leona Maricle
Gloria Hamilton	Kay Sutton
Mr. Thomas	Miles Mander
Subway Watchman	John Qualen
D.A.'s Secretary	Grady Sutton
Mr. X.	Olin Howland

CREDITS:

Screenplay by	Philip G. Epstein
Story by	Wilson Collinson
Producer	Pandro S. Berman
Director	Leigh Jason
Associate Producer	P. J. Wolfson
Photographed by	Nicholas Musuraca, A.S.C.
Art Director	Van Nest Polglase
Associate Art Director	Carroll Clark
Set Dressing by	Darrell Silvera
Gowns by	Edward Stevenson
Recorded by	Richard Van Hessen
Assistant Director	Edward Donahue
Edited by	George Hively

THE MAD MISS MANTON

FADE IN

EXTERIOR FASHIONABLE APARTMENT HOUSE—NIGHT
Medium shot—shooting from curb. At the corner is a half-built subway entrance to a still-unused subway; cement mixers are standing on the curb, barrels of cement, rolls of tar paper, etc. A limousine draws up outside of the apartment house. A liveried chauffeur gets out from the front seat and opens the rear door. Melsa Manton, in her attractive middle twenties, gets out. One quality about Melsa is at once evident—even at this hour in the morning. She is pert, sparkling, alive. She wears an evening cloak over some sort of costume—exactly what it is we cannot tell at the moment.

MELSA: Good night, James.
JAMES: Good night, Miss Manton.
Melsa starts up the curb toward the apartment house. James tips his hat and returns to the car. He gets in and drives off. As Melsa approaches the apartment house door, it opens and the doorman emerges with six Pomeranians on their respective leashes. The dogs all make a mad dash for Melsa, hopping and jumping all over her.

1

*She gathers as many as she can into her arms and starts cooing at
them.*

MELSA: *(to the six Pomeranians, en masse)* Hello, you darlings. Are you
all here? Did you miss mama?

One little Pomeranian makes a special jump at her.

DOORMAN: Three o'clock, Miss Manton—right on time. I went right up
after you called. I had to wake your maid. Boy, was she fried—er, I mean
angry!

MELSA: *(getting dogs together)* If I know Hilda, she was *fried,* not
angry! *(to the dogs)* Remember, you're out here for exercise—no
loafing!

*As Melsa begins to pass the subway excavation, a piece of tar paper
clings to one of the dogs' paws.*

MELSA: *(continued)* What's the matter, Tiger? *(she stoops to remove tar
paper)* Here, Tiger, stand still—that's the sweet boy—*(she looks at
paper)* There seems to be no justice for dogs, Tiger—you suffer through
the building of the subway and when it's finished they won't even let you
in—now when I'm president, I'll build subways for dogs and won't let
humans in. *(she straightens up)* All right, gentlemen, let's walk.

She continues walking down the street.

EXTERIOR BROWNSTONE HOUSE—NIGHT

*It is a few houses down the street from the apartment house. The
windows are all boarded up. There is a "For Sale" sign in one of the
windows, and the general appearance of the house is one of long
disuse. We see Melsa coming up the street with the dogs some
distance from the house. Suddenly the door of the old house opens
and a man in evening dress, his coat collar up over his ears, his face
slumped into his coat, comes out of the house and starts walking
quickly down the steps.*

EXTERIOR STREET—NIGHT

*Melsa gazes in the direction of the house. As she sees the man
coming down the steps, her face looks puzzled, then a look of
recognition comes over it. She calls out.*

MELSA: Ronnie!

EXTERIOR HOUSE—NIGHT

The man hurries down the steps, giving no sign that he has heard or seen Melsa. Reaching the sidewalk, he hurries off toward the corner, his figure being silhouetted against the walls of the houses as he passes the street lamps. He disappears around the corner. Melsa comes into scene, looks in the direction the man has disappeared. She is still apparently puzzled. The six dogs start whining and tug away from her. Melsa looks inquiringly at the dogs, then up at the house. It is evident to her that the dogs, sensing something in the house, want to get away from it. She ties the dogs to the railing of the stoop, then slowly, with not too much courage, walks up the steps. At the door, she hesitates for a moment, takes a deep breath, then turns the knob and exits into the house.

INTERIOR FOYER—HOUSE—NIGHT

The door slowly creaks open and Melsa enters. We barely see her in the darkness. She takes out a cigarette lighter and, after a few nervous attempts, lights it. As far as we can see in the dim light, the foyer is dusty and the few pieces of furniture are covered. Melsa gazes around her, starts walking forward slowly, her lips trembling a little. As she walks, her foot strikes something. She stops and bends down, and the flame of the cigarette lighter shows us a diamond clip lying on the floor. Melsa bends down and picks it up. As she examines it, we can see that it is a very expensive clip. Melsa puts the clip in her cloak pocket, looks around, then advances slowly towards the next room. She listens at the door for a moment, then gathering up her reserve courage slowly opens the door and exits into the room.

INTERIOR LIVING ROOM—HOUSE—NIGHT

It is in the same condition as the foyer except that there is much more furniture, all similarly covered. Melsa enters the room, gazes around, starts a few steps forward, then she stops and her eyes widen and her mouth pops open. She starts to emit a scream but nothing comes out. Camera pans with Melsa's horrified gaze down to the floor where we see a man lying stretched out on his stomach. We can see very little of his face except that from his temple down

3

what we can see of his face is covered with blood. He is dressed in evening clothes.

Medium shot—Melsa starts forward, thinks a bit, stops, starts forward again, then decides that she is no heroine and turns and starts running out of the room. As she passes the door, her cape gets caught on the door. Melsa runs out, leaving the cape, and we now see that she is dressed in a baby outfit.

INTERIOR FOYER—HOUSE—NIGHT
Melsa comes dashing in, making a beeline for the front door.

EXTERIOR HOUSE—NIGHT
Shooting up toward the steps. Melsa comes out, clambers down the steps, unties the dogs, and dashes down the street. At the corner, she stops and looks around for a policeman, then dashes down a side street.

EXTERIOR SIDE STREET—NIGHT
Melsa comes running into scene, still looking for a policeman. She sees a police box at the corner. She stops at the box, opens it, and pulls the lever. She makes a strange picture as she waits on the street corner in her costume, holding onto the six straining Pomeranians. A cab drives by. The heads of the driver and two occupants pop out of the cab. They continue staring as the cab drives down the street. The cab starts swerving towards the curb and only quick action by the driver saves it from crashing on the sidewalk.

DISSOLVE

EXTERIOR SIDE STREET—NIGHT
Melsa is standing on the corner. The sirens of police cars are heard and three police cars dash up to the box. Lieutenant Brent, a nervous, dyspeptic type (Sam Levene), leans out of the car and looks at Melsa in her costume. He is just as amazed as the rest of his confreres in the cars.

BRENT: Is the dress too short or are you too long?

MELSA: *(stutteringly)* No, I was just...

4

BRENT: Did you see anybody phone from the police box?

MELSA: I did!

BRENT: What is this—a gag?

MELSA: *(excitedly)* No, sir. I was at a costume party—
She becomes irrelevant in her excitement.

MELSA: *(continued)* It was on 14th Street off Second—an artists' ball—I had to hit a man because he tried to kiss me—I—I mean, the door was open and I walked in and he was lying there in a pool of blood—his own.

BRENT: *(rasping)* That's no reason—killing a man because he tried to kiss you.

MELSA: It isn't the same man, and I didn't kill him.

BRENT: *(irascibly)* Well, come on, get in, get in!
Melsa climbs into the car, taking the dogs with her. The dogs start climbing all over the members of the homocide squad, adding to the confusion. The car starts off.

DISSOLVE

EXTERIOR STREET—OUTSIDE HOUSE—NIGHT
The other cars draw up behind Brent's car and the men start piling out. Melsa gets out, holding onto her dogs. The dogs start whining and pulling at their leashes.

MELSA: *(to Brent)* You see. They know there's somebody dead in there.

BRENT: *(in amazement)* And you dragged us out on that evidence!

MELSA: Oh, no. I saw him myself—but everybody knows that when dogs know somebody's dead, they howl. These dogs can't howl, but if they could, they'd howl.

BRENT: *(controlling his temper)* Lady, just show us the corpse, will you?
He starts up the steps, followed by the policemen. Melsa ties the dogs to the railing of the stoop and hurries after Brent. At the top of the steps, she stops him.

MELSA: Now, wait a minute, Inspector.

BRENT: *(sourly)* Lieutenant—Lieutenant Brent.

MELSA: Shouldn't you send two men around the rear of the house?

BRENT: What for? The guy's dead, isn't he?

MELSA: But the murderer might still be in there.
Brent makes a visible effort to control himself.

5

BRENT: Look, lady, it's ten minutes since you called us, and the murderer—if there is a murderer—could be in Brooklyn by now; that is, if anybody wants to be in Brooklyn! Now, let's take a look at the body.

He turns and opens the door. A policeman behind him, gun drawn, in his eagerness to get in almost steps on Brent.

BRENT: *(continued) (to policeman)* Quit climbing up on me—and watch out where you're pointing that gun!

They enter.

INTERIOR FOYER—HOUSE—NIGHT

Brent, the policemen, and Melsa are walking slowly down the foyer.

BRENT: *(to Melsa)* Do you know whose house this is?

MELSA: It's the old Lane mansion. He's a banker. We know him—his wife, too—she's a nice girl—she's twenty years nicer than he is—I mean younger.

BRENT: Pull yourself together.

MELSA: *(teeth chattering)* This is my first murder.

BRENT: *(doubtingly)* Do you know it was murder the same way your dogs do?

MELSA: I'm only trying to help.

BRENT: Can you identify the corpse?

MELSA: I couldn't see his face because he was lying on his stomach and I didn't want to turn him over because, you know, Inspector, you mustn't touch a corpse until the police come.

She looks at Brent thoughtfully.

MELSA: *(continued)* You ought to know. *(indicating the door)* In that room.

Her expression changes, and we see the courage leaving her face.

MELSA: *(continued)* And if you don't mind, I—I'll run along now. I—

She makes a gesture of distaste, pointing toward the room.

BRENT: Sorry, lady, but we'll have to ask you to hang around.

A policeman opens the door and they all start in.

INTERIOR LIVING ROOM—NIGHT

Brent, policemen, and Melsa enter and gaze around. The room is exactly as we left it—except that there is no body on the floor.

6

There is a significant moment of silence. The policemen gaze at each other. Melsa looks at the door and sees that her cape is gone. Utterly bewildered, she sinks into a chair.

MELSA: Well, what do you think about that?

BRENT: *(menacingly)* Lady, I know what *I'm* thinking. What are *you* thinking, that's what I want to know?

MELSA: *(stammering)* But—but—I saw it—I swear to you! He was dead! And my cloak—it was on the door—and now it isn't!

The policemen exchange significant looks, then advance slowly on Melsa from all sides.

BRENT: Now, lady, you mustn't be frightened. Don't get excited. You're among friends. We've a nice, quiet place in the country—

Suddenly he bends down and with the side of his hand hits Melsa right below the knee. Her leg jerks upward. Brent turns disappointedly to the policemen.

BRENT: *(continued)* She's not nuts!

MELSA: *(earnestly)* I'm not crazy, I tell you.

BRENT: *(wheeling on her)* What kind of a game are you playing? What's your name?

MELSA: Manton—Melsa Manton.

BRENT: *(his expression changing)* Oh—Melsa Manton, eh? Aren't you one of the bunch that held a treasure hunt last week and stole a traffic signal?

MELSA: *(nodding weakly)* Yes, but it was a treasure hunt for charity. We run a T.B. clinic.

BRENT: And aren't you the dame who got an ambulance from Bellevue because one of your dogs had distemper?

MELSA: *(protesting)* Well, he was very sick and the veterinarian was out of town.

BRENT: *(his fury mounting)* And aren't you the dame who—?

MELSA: Yes.

Brent struggles with himself. His face contorts with pain. He taps his stomach, pantomiming that all is not well there. Finally, he manages to talk to one of the policemen.

BRENT: Give me them stomach tablets.

POLICEMAN: *(reaching in his coat)* Coming up, Chief.

MELSA: *(her brow wrinkling in nervousness)* There's a murderer loose, I tell you, and he's got my cloak!

BRENT: *(unimpressed)* Don't worry, it won't fit him! Now go on home before I call a truant officer.

MELSA: *(protesting)* Please, please, believe me...

BRENT: *(interrupting)* Miss Manton, I don't know what your game is but I know this—either your education or your spanking has been neglected. I can't do anything about spanking you. *(reflectively)* Or can I?

MELSA: Don't you dare!

BRENT: But I can do something about your education as far as the police are concerned. We are a completely democratic organization, Miss Manton, sworn to uphold the law and administer it equally to all. We are at the beck and call of every citizen who may need us. This time we were glad to come but if you involve the police department in one more of your merry peccadillos I'll lock you up so tight you'll need a major earthquake to get you out, and now run along home and count your money.

Melsa, incensed, rises. She is almost crying.

MELSA: *(tears in her eyes)* All right, all right. There *was* a body and I reported it; my duty's been done. Now the police department can go its smug and snide and... and illiterate way. If I ever see another murder, before I report it, I hope... I hope... I hope I'm the victim.

She slams her hat on and storms out.

OFFICER: And I always wanted to marry a rich dame.

BRENT: If you promise to beat her every day, I'll arrange it... Come on, boys.

They begin to exit.

DISSOLVE

INTERIOR NEWSPAPER OFFICE—DAY
Close up of a newspaper story on the editorial page, headed

THE MAD MISS MANTON
THROWS ANOTHER FIT

THE DAFFY GROUP AGAIN INVOLVES
POLICE IN SENSELESS ESCAPADE

8

by
Peter Ames

Camera pulls back to reveal that the paper is held by Peter Ames, a rather youngish-looking man for his position of editor. He is seated behind a desk, another man seated at the side of the desk.

MAN: We've got forty telegrams commending your article.

PETER: That's fine. Take another one. *(he starts pacing and dictating)* "We'd like to preface this editorial with the statement that Wall Street hit another low today. Unemployment reached another peak. An additional four billion dollars was added to the budget. But Miss Manton and her ilk—Helen Frayne, Myra Frost, Dora Fenton, Pat James, Lee Wilson, Kit Beverly—go merrily on in the same million-dollar, ermine-lined way. *(afterthought)* By the bye, according to the police, Miss Manton looked fetching in her costume. *(he takes a few more paces, then continues)* At a time when our city calls for service from its citizens, for constructive cooperation—at such a time does the mad Miss Manton choose to involve the police department in an escapade. It seems to me—"

The door flies open and Melsa storms in. Both men get up as Melsa enters. She walks up to the man who had been seated at the side of the desk and, without warning, slaps him full in the face.

MELSA: *(to the man)* Are you Peter Ames?

MAN: No.

MELSA: Sorry.

Melsa turns to Peter and slaps him. There is a bit of a tableau for awhile until Peter turns to Melsa.

PETER: *(calmly)* To complete the circle.

He slaps Melsa. She slumps into a chair and starts to weep. Peter walks over to her.

PETER: *(continued)* Now that we've met, will you tell me why a perfect stranger dashes into my office and slaps another perfect stranger in the face?

MAN: *(holding his face)* How about me? Two perfect strangers.

Melsa doesn't say anything, but continues weeping.

PETER: *(to man, dismissing him)* All right, John.

The man leaves.

9

Close shot. Peter walks over to Melsa and bends over her.

PETER: *(continued) (apologetically)* I'm awfully sorry, Miss. I don't as a rule go around hitting women—that is, not as often as I'd like to. It was pure reflex—self-preservation and all that. *(handing her a handkerchief)* Will you please stop crying?

MELSA: *(taking the handkerchief and dabbing at her eyes)* I'm not crying—I'm just mad. *(handing him the newspaper)* Did you write this awful thing?

PETER: *(glancing at the editorial)* Yes. *(he looks at her)* Oh, you're Melsa Manton.

> *She nods. Peter's expression changes. His tone becomes brusque. He takes the handkerchief from her.*

PETER: *(continued) (as he snatches the handkerchief from her)* Laundry is quite an item to me.

> *He walks back to his desk, and his manner becomes businesslike.*

PETER: *(continued)* I'm a very busy man, Miss Manton.

MELSA: How dare you print such offensive innuendos.

PETER: *(coldly)* It isn't a question of courage. It's a question of convictions—of policy.

MELSA: I see. And who decides that policy?

PETER: Well, newspapers are funny institutions. They take an ordinary reporter like me and make him an editor—as long as he's willing to work for the same salary. Every time you ask for a raise, they promote you. The first time, they gave me my name on the door. The second time, they let me decide on policy—at least, in matters like this.

> *Melsa looks coldly at Peter, then gets up, walks to the door and calls out.*

MELSA: Mr. Spengler!

> *Medium shot. After a moment a middle-aged man with no particular characteristics evident enters the office.*

MELSA: *(continued)* Mr. Ames, I want you to meet a friend of mine, Mr. Spengler.

PETER: *(fiddling with some papers on his desk)* If I weren't so busy, I'd be charmed. Now, if both of you will excuse—

> *Spengler walks over to Peter and hands him a paper.*

SPENGLER: Here's the summons, Mr. Ames—I hope you don't take this personal.

Peter reads the summons.

SPENGLER: *(continued)* I read your paper regular, and I agree with you. Miss Manton here is all wrong.

Melsa goes over to Spengler and hands him a bill.

MELSA: That will be all, Mr. Spengler, thank you.

Peter is still reading through the summons. Spengler exits. Peter looks up from the summons and whistles grimly.

PETER: A million dollars for libel! *(sarcastically)* Coupled with your present income, won't that send your income tax away up in the surtax brackets?

MELSA: Don't worry about it. I'll give it to charity. *(making a face)* And don't speak to me about income tax.

They stand facing each other antagonistically. Finally, Peter takes a different tack.

PETER: This is all very silly. You haven't a leg to stand on—*(looking at her legs)*—figuratively speaking. That editorial just stated facts. You *did* disrupt the police department. There *wasn't* a corpse.

MELSA: *(emphatically, sincerely)* There *was* a corpse, and I'll prove it, if I have to find the body myself.

She walks to the door.

PETER: You sound as if you contemplate committing murder.

Melsa stops at the door, turns and looks pointedly at Peter.

MELSA: *(coldly)* I have someone in mind right now!

PETER: *(bowing grimly)* At your service.

Melsa exits. Peter's face reveals a troubled frown. He thinks for a moment, then goes to the office Dictograph and speaks through it.

PETER: *(continued)* Get me our attorneys—at once!

DISSOLVE OUT

DISSOLVE IN

INTERIOR MANTON LIVING ROOM—NIGHT

The room is cluttered with a group of girls in evening dress. Melsa is pacing up and down the room telling a story. One of the girls, Pat James, is busy nibbling a sandwich and sipping coffee. Dora, a vacant-looking young miss, stares intently. All the girls are more or

11

less attractive. Helen Frayne, a bit more intelligent-looking than the rest, queries Melsa.

HELEN: Why didn't you slap him?

MELSA: I did and his reflex slapped me right back.

DORA: I don't think that was very gentlemanly. Now, down South—

HELEN: *(interrupting)* I know—they hit you with fried chicken.

MELSA: *(to Helen)* Stop razzing Dora. He's no gentleman—and we're going to prove it in court.

MYRA: Let's boycott their society editor. We won't send them any more pictures of ourselves.

Dora bites nails. Helen slaps her hand. (Keep as running gag.)

MELSA: We can't sit back complacently and let them ridicule us.

LEE: *(a languorous type stretched out comfortably in an easy chair)* They might occasionally mention some of the good we do.

MELSA: That isn't the point. There's no truth in that stuff he printed and it's up to us as a group to prove it.

HELEN: I've always wanted to pound a picket line.

KIT: Now, Melsa, do you remember the night you saw Queen Elizabeth in all her clothes taking a bath in your own tub?

MELSA: Are you suggesting I had too many absinthe frappés?

LEE: We must exhaust all possibilities before we devote all our lives to a corpse hunt.

PAT: After all, darling, you're the only one who says there was a murder.

MELSA: I *did* see the body and my cloak certainly didn't run off by itself.

DORA: Maybe the body wasn't dead.

MELSA: It was lying on its stomach.

KIT: Which means I've been dead for twenty-three years!

HELEN: Twenty-seven, dear.

KIT: Or thereabouts.

MELSA: *(bringing out some flashlights)* Here are some flashlights. We're all going over to the Lane house tonight. I'll prove I'm not crazy!

HELEN: You can't prove it with flashlights.

MYRA: *(plaintively)* I can't go tonight—got a date. Can't we prove you're not crazy some other night?

HELEN: *(sarcastically)* Sure, we'll ask the murderer not to touch a thing!

MELSA: I was away for ten minutes, and the corpse sneaked out.

12

Hilda, a large—a very *large—black maid enters, or rather, wobbles into the room.*

HILDA: Telephone for you, Miss Frost.

Myra runs for the phone.

MYRA: *(exclaiming)* That's my date!

HILDA: *(unimpressed)* He sho' sounded lak a pipsqueak to me.

Hilda walks over to the ashtrays and starts emptying them. Myra takes the phone and lies down seductively on the sofa.

Close shot.

MYRA: *(into phone, softly)* Hello, Paul—no, dear, I can't—no, just a minute. *(putting her hand over the mouthpiece, and turning to the girls)* Please . . .

MELSA: No, we've got to do it tonight.

MYRA: *(pleadingly)* But you should hear how he sounds.

MELSA: According to Hilda, he sounds like a pipsqueak.

MYRA: A lot she knows about pipsqueaks. *(into phone)* Hello, pipsqueak—no, I mean, dear—no, no—honestly . . .

One of the girls pulls out the jack plug.

MYRA: *(continued) (into phone)* Hello—hello, dear—are you there?

She hangs up and turns to the girls.

MYRA: *(continued)* He was cut off.

HELEN: Poor boy—and in the prime of his life, too.

Medium shot. Hilda is walking by Pat.

PAT: Have you got any more cake, Hilda?

HILDA: Yes, ma'am, Ah have, but de kitchen is closed for de night.

MELSA: Hilda! Miss Beverly is our guest.

HILDA: Ah didn't ask her up.

The doorbell rings. Hilda pays no attention to it.

MELSA: Hilda, the door.

HILDA: *(shuffling off toward door)* Ah heard it—Ah ain't deaf. Sometimes Ah wish Ah was!

HELEN: Comes the revolution, we'll stop being exploited by our help.

MELSA: *(looking off after Hilda)* In *my* house, the revolution is here!

Medium close shot. Hilda comes back into the room accompanied by a telegraph messenger boy.

BOY: I was told to deliver this to Miss Manton personally. Sender requests an answer.

13

Melsa holds out her hand and takes the telegram. She opens it and reads aloud.

MELSA: *(reading)* "May I come up to see you tonight? Just want half hour of your time. Peter Ames." *(turning to girls)* That's the newspaper editor.

HELEN: Let him up. We'll play mumbley-peg in his back.

MELSA: *(turning to boy)* The answer is "no."

BOY: In that case, here's another telegram for you.

Melsa, surprised, takes the second wire, opens it and reads it.

MELSA: *(reading)* "I'm coming up anyway. Peter Ames."

The messenger boy stands staring ogle-eyed at the girls. Hilda taps him on the arm.

HILDA: Okay, chile.

She ushers the boy out of the room.

HILDA: *(continued)* You'd think dey'd send an older man up to dis heah apartment.

The girls all have their flashlights in their hands.

MELSA: All right, come on, girls. Hilda, will you get the girls' wraps?

Hilda exits. The girls get up and start getting ready to leave.

HELEN: What happens if the Lanes drop in while we're snooping around?

MELSA: The house is for sale—they've lived at a hotel for a year.

KIT: You mean they've quarrelled at a hotel for a year.

HELEN: *(to Kit)* I don't know which is more pernicious, you or anemia.

MELSA: I'll call their hotel and check. *(she dials phone)* What'll I say?

DORA: Say, hello—

MELSA: Thanks, Dora, you're sweet—and very helpful. *(into phone)* Mr. Lane, please . . . What? . . . Oh. Well, then, Mrs. Lane . . . Oh, did she? Did she take a bag? Oh, thank you. *(hanging up phone and turning to girls)* George Lane is out of town. Sheila left yesterday after dinner—asked her butler to prepare a midnight snack, and then didn't come home. Hasn't been home since.

Hilda is now in the room and is helping the girls on with their coats.

LEE: Do you suppose she's skipped with Ronnie Belden? You've heard about those two—

HELEN: Remind me when I have time to wash your mouth with soap and water.

14

MELSA: Illegal entry or no illegal entry, we're entering the Lane house tonight, then we'll pay a call on Mr. Ronnie Belden.

The doorbell rings.

PAT: There's your editor.

MELSA: *(to the girls)* Duck your flashlights.

They put their flashlights under their coats. Melsa and the girls start for the door.

MELSA: *(continued)* Remember, girls, I want the first stab at him.

PAT: I want to twist the knife.

INTERIOR FOYER—MANTON APARTMENT—NIGHT

The girls enter.

MELSA: *(to Hilda)* I'll open the door, Hilda. *(as she strides to the door; vindictively)* I'll fix him!

She swings the door open quickly. There, stuck to the door, is her cloak, a knife through it, and a note under the knife. The girls gasp.

MELSA: *(continued) (gasping)* My cloak!

Melsa looks at the note and reads aloud.

MELSA: *(continued) (reading)* "The next time you'll be in it."

The girls stifle their shrieks. Melsa hurriedly slams the door shut.

MELSA: *(continued) (her voice choked with excitement)* The murderer's been here!

MYRA: *(moaning)* Why didn't I keep that date?

PAT: What'll we do?

HELEN: I don't know. I can't think.

Dora bites nails. Gets slapped.

MELSA: We can't show the white feather. This is our chance. *(she turns on them)* Don't you want to justify yourselves?

KIT: If I can stay alive doing it, yes—If not, *no!*

DORA: I'm with you, Melsa. I prefer death to dishonor. That's a Southern code.

HELEN: *(in a fierce whisper)* Quiet, Dora—he may be a Yankee.

DORA: *(innocently)* Why, I'm sure he is.

HILDA: *(to Melsa scoldingly)* Dat knife ain't for openin' lettahs. You look heah—you-all stay home and don' go messin' 'round in things what ain't none of yo' business. If somebody wants to go 'round murderin' folks, 'tain't none of yo' concern!

MELSA: *(her chin out)* You think any of this stuff is going to intimidate me? It's all the more reason—

There is a loud, imperative knocking on the door. All the girls look at each other, scared.

LEE: *(in a whisper)* Oh, who can that be?

MYRA: *(in a low moan)* I wish Paul were here—I want Paul.

DORA: *(in a quaking whisper)* I want my mother!

HELEN: I'll settle for a policeman! A strong policeman.

Dora bites nails, reminds herself, desists. Melsa hefts the flashlight in her hand like a blackjack and signals to Kit to open the door. Hilda strides to the door and opens it. Peter, the cloak hanging over one arm and the knife held in his other hand, stands in the doorway. Melsa's flashlight stops in mid-air.

PETER: *(indicating the knife and cloak)* Very nice props, but it doesn't convince me. Now, suppose you send this knife back to the kitchen, and—whichever one of you wrote this note—"you'll" is spelled with two "L's." Sorry, I'm not gullible.

MELSA: *(stuttering in her anger)* You—you fool—you big fool! You ruined the fingerprints!

PETER: Did I? Well, I can get you plenty of other fingerprints. Miss Manton, I came up to see whether I couldn't talk you out of this childishness. You can't possibly win, but it's bound to be a lot of trouble for us—and for yourself.

Melsa snatches the cloak and knife from Peter, puts the knife in her coat pocket, and tosses the cloak to Hilda. She turns to Peter.

MELSA: *(coldly)* If any of us girls is in trouble, we know what to do about it. *(to girls)* Come along, girls.

Full shot as the girls start down the hall.

MYRA: *(looking back over her shoulder at Peter)* He's cute!

Peter stares after them, as

DISSOLVE

EXTERIOR STREET OUTSIDE LANE HOUSE—NIGHT

The girls come into scene. Myra hesitates, obviously afraid to go up.

MELSA: *(walking defiantly up the steps)* They're always accusing us of being parasites. This is our chance to prove we're of some use in the community.

The girls follow after Melsa.

HELEN: This is your brain child, Lady Macbeth. Lead on!

Melsa reaches for the door and tries to open it, but it is locked. She rattles it and tries to push it open, but it remains closed. She turns to the girls.

MELSA: Locked! I guess the police fixed it. *(petulantly)* Why don't they mind their own business?

DORA: Ah don' reckon they wan' us to go in!

MYRA: *(heaving a sigh of relief)* We've done our duty to the community for tonight.

PAT: Well, you can't say we never tried.

Melsa, however, refuses to quit. Next to the door there is a double French window with a little balcony in front of it. Melsa climbs over the railing and starts removing the boards that cover one window. Turning to the girls.

MELSA: C'mon—it's open!

INTERIOR LANE LIVING ROOM—NIGHT

As the girls file into the room. They begin flashing their lights up and down the room.

MELSA: This is the room. Go over it with a fine-tooth comb.

The girls start searching around.

MELSA: *(continued)* I found the clip out in the foyer. There might be some other things lying around—bloodstains, maybe fingerprints, or things knocked over in the struggle.

Pat's searchlight flashes onto a box of candy. Pat reaches in it, comes up with a chocolate, and starts munching on it. Over in another corner, Myra, with the aid of her flashlight, has found a telephone. Melsa comes running over to her.

MELSA: *(continued)* What on earth are you doing?

MYRA: I'm calling Paul.

Melsa slaps the receiver out of her hand.

LEE: *(pointing to ink)* Look! Blood!

All the girls come running over excitedly.

MELSA: How can it be blood? It's blue.

17

HELEN: Maybe they shot Mrs. Astor.

PAT: It's ink. Somebody spilled a bottle of ink.

MELSA: *(turning to Helen)* Helen, you search the upstairs.

HELEN: *(shaking her head)* I was never much of an individualist. If the upstairs has to be searched, we'll search it together.

DORA: That's communism!

> They hear a door slam. The girls stiffen in their fright. Their eyes pop open.

MELSA: *(whispering)* Turn off your flashlights.

DORA: *(whispering)* Please, can't I keep mine on? I'm scared of the dark.

MELSA: *(in a hurried whisper)* If you don't turn it off, you won't live to see the dark. Stand against the wall. When he comes in, pounce on him.

> The girls walk towards the walls and flatten themselves against them. The door opens slowly and a man stands silhouetted in the doorway. He peers around the room and steps slowly into the room. His hand gropes for the light on the wall. Dora, who is standing next to the light fixture, starts edging away from it. However, the man's hand finally connects up with her and grasps her arm. Dora lets out a scream. All the girls fall on the man. In the dark we see a struggle going on.

AD LIBS: Grab him! Grab him!

MAN'S VOICE: Leggo! Leggo, I tell you!

AD LIBS: Hold his leg!

That's my leg, you dope!

MAN'S VOICE: Hey, what is this?

AD LIBS: Ouch!

Strike a woman, will you!

Ouch!

What's the matter?

I bit myself!

Tie him up!

What'll we tie him with?

Here—here's something.

Need some more!

Coming up—there, that's it!

That'll hold him!

> The flashlights go on, revealing Peter. He is all tied up, women's

18

stockings around his legs and arms, a sash around his waist, women's undergarments binding other parts of him. Myra is sitting on his chest. Melsa gives Peter a long, vindictive look.

MELSA: *(to Myra)* Don't be a pig, Myra—move over. *(she sits down next to Myra, and gives Peter a satisfied glance)* Got worried, didn't you? Thought there might be something in my story, after all.

One girl's belt off—skirt always slipping down. Follow through with next scene.

PETER: *(with quiet venom)* You dressmaker's dummies are going to rue the night you laid a hand on Peter Ames!

MYRA: *(looking Peter over)* I still think he's cute. *(quickly, to Melsa)* I mean no disloyalty to you, Melsa.

HELEN: *(holds her nose)* Nosebleed!

MELSA: Get something cold—a key. Who's got a key?

PAT: How about his wrist watch?

They take it off him.

PETER: That's grand larceny! I'll take care of you girls for this.

MYRA: You darling—how nice of you. *(she kisses him)*

MELSA: That's petty larceny!

The watch falls through dress and shatters.

MELSA: *(continued)* So sorry. *(getting up and speaking briskly to the girls)* Come on, girls, we've got more business.

The girls follow her as she starts out.

MYRA: *(plaintively)* Not any more tonight—Paul's waiting.

DORA: You can't do that. We've got to go to Ronnie Belden's.

Melsa kicks her.

DORA: *(continued) (with a backward glance at Peter)* Are we going to leave him here?

MELSA: He'll be all right. They'll probably tear these buildings down in twenty or thirty years... it will take him that long to mellow.

They exit. Peter starts straining at his ties, as we

DISSOLVE OUT

DISSOLVE IN

19

INTERIOR APARTMENT HOUSE CORRIDOR—NIGHT

It is a very lovely corridor, obviously in a very expensive, luxurious apartment house. The girls come tripping down the hall—camera trucking with them.

LEE: It's apartment 701.

MELSA: *(looking at her suspiciously)* How do you know?

LEE: I found his keys once—*(the girls look at her)*—and mailed them right back to him.

MELSA: Let me do the questioning. Mr. Belden has a lot of explaining to do. He can't cut me dead in the street—even if he was running away from a murder! *(she rings doorbell)*

MYRA: But it's got to be cleared up by tomorrow. I just can't disappoint Paul again.

The girls wait for someone to come to the door. After a moment, Melsa knocks on the door. They wait a moment. Still no one answers the door. Melsa rings the bell again. A waiter passes by with a tray of food. Pat's eyes and heart follow the waiter as he proceeds down the hall with a tray. Melsa impatiently tries the door. It swings open. The girls look at each other in surprise.

MELSA: It's—it's unlocked.

She steps in, reaches out and snaps on the light in the vestibule, then walks in the apartment, followed by the girls.

DORA: It doesn't seem right to go into a man's apartment without a chaperone!

INTERIOR BELDEN APARTMENT LIVING ROOM—NIGHT

It is a large room furnished in expensive good taste. The girls file into the room and look around. Nothing seems to be disturbed.

MELSA: *(calling)* Ronnie—Ronnie!

There is no reply.

MELSA: *(continued) (to the girls)* Doesn't seem to be here. Well, let's see what we can find, anyway. There might be a gun around.

The girls start searching. Pat, Lee, and Kit go into different rooms. Melsa is searching around; Pat, Lee, and Kit re-enter the room and walk over to the others.

KIT: Couldn't find a thing.

20

LEE: Nothing exciting in the bedroom.

Pat slips away from the group and starts toward the kitchen.

INTERIOR BELDEN APARTMENT KITCHEN—NIGHT

It is a large, spacious room with all modern improvements. Pat enters and starts prowling around. She sees a sandwich on a tray, goes to it, and picks it up. She then crosses to the stove and lights the burner under a percolator sitting on top of the stove. She crosses to the cupboard, opens it, and takes a cup off the shelf. She looks into the cup and suddenly calls out in surprise.

PAT: *(calling)* Hey, girls! Look at this!

The girls come running into the room.

Pat turns the cup over and a clip falls into her hand. The girls gasp.

MELSA: *(snatching the clip)* Give it to me. *(examining it)* It's the same!

LEE: It's Sheila's. They had a picture of it in last month's *Fashion Parade.*

Pat, whose attention has been divided between the clip and the food, is cutting a slice of bread.

MELSA: I put that clip in my cloak last night. When I went to call the police, Ronnie must have gone back, taken the body and my cloak. *(she gets an idea)* Wait a minute!

She takes the knife from her coat, goes over to the silverware drawer, opens it, and takes out another knife.

Close shot—of the two knives. They are obviously from the same set.

Medium group shot.

MELSA: *(continued)* Well, I guess it's Ronnie, all right.

LEE: *(unbelieving)* Ronnie, a murderer?

DORA: Gee, and I had him to tea!

MELSA: *(now the great sleuth)* You see, I'm different—I can't be fooled where a man's character is concerned. I knew there was something shifty about him.

Pat walks over to the large refrigerator, opens the door, and suddenly screams at the top of her voice, slumping to the floor in a faint. The girls all turn to the refrigerator.

Close shot of the refrigerator. Ronnie, his eyes glassy in death, a

*knife sticking in his chest, is wedged in the refrigerator.
Group shot. The girls shriek.*

HELEN: It's Ronnie Belden!

*They make a dash for the living room, leaving Pat lying on the
floor, still in her faint.*

INTERIOR BELDEN LIVING ROOM—NIGHT
The girls dash in. Melsa stops.

MELSA: Wait a minute. We've got to go in and get Pat.

AD LIBS: Not me!

You can't get me in there! *etc., etc.*

Melsa, with a scornful look at the girls, goes into the kitchen.

DORA: *(gazing after her)* Isn't Melsa brave?

LEE: And we all thought Ronnie Belden did it!

KIT: I got a psychic feeling we're all marked for slaughter.

*Melsa enters, dragging Pat, who is still unconscious. The girls go to
her and help her drag Pat to a couch.*

MELSA: *(scornfully)* There you are. Afraid of a dead man! Why, I—

Suddenly she falls in a faint to the floor.

DISSOLVE

INTERIOR BELDEN LIVING ROOM—NIGHT
Melsa is at the phone.

MELSA: *(into phone)* Inspector Brent, please—Homicide.

*Camera pans with her gaze across the room as she turns to the girls.
The girls are grouped around Pat, who is still lying on the couch.*

MELSA'S VOICE: *(continued) (off-scene)* Hasn't she come to yet?

KIT: Melsa, you know that she's more delicate than you.

*Pat's eyelids start to flutter. Slowly she opens her eyes, then
automatically takes a bite out of the bread in her hand.*

HELEN: She'll be all right now—she's got food in her mouth.

Close shot—Melsa at phone.

MELSA: *(into phone, impatiently)* Yes, Inspector Brent—and hurry,
please... Miss Manton—

INTERIOR BOOKING ROOM—POLICE HEADQUARTERS— NIGHT

Lieutenant Brent and a half dozen policemen are crossing the room. Brent is talking to the men.

BRENT: You'll break into the joint sharp on the hour. Don't bother with the guests. Just get the croupiers. And remember, I don't want to find any chips in your vest pockets.

As they pass the sergeant's desk, the sergeant calls out to Brent.

SERGEANT: Oh, Lieutenant—

Brent and the men stop.

SERGEANT: *(continued)* There's a dame wants to speak to you on the phone.

BRENT: A dame?

He cannot resist a look of satisfaction that his men are hearing this.

SERGEANT: Yeah—says her name's Manton.

Brent's face falls.

BRENT: *(in a disgusted tone)* Manton! Tell that dame—gimme that phone!

He snatches the phone, then calls out to one of his men:

BRENT: *(continued)* Mac, get that bicarb tablet ready.

MAC: Coming up.

BRENT: *(into phone)* Look here, Miss Manton, *we* realize that we're public servants—*(his voice gets louder)*—but do *you* realize it? *(his voice softens with sarcasm)* Oh, you found another body? Uh-huh, I see ... Well, I'll tell you what to do—keep it on ice, see? *(his face grows apoplectic)* What!!! It *IS* on ice!!!! *(his voice becomes violent)* Now, look here, Miss Manton, get out of my life, do you hear? *(trembling with rage and shrieking into the phone)* GET—OUT—OF—MY—LIFE!!!!

EXTERIOR MORNING CLARION NEWSPAPER BUILD-ING—NIGHT

A taxi draws up the curb. Peter gets out. He is disheveled, his clothes awry, his hair mussed. He pays the driver and walks to the building, rubbing his wrists. A newsboy stands at the corner calling out headlines.

NEWSBOY: *(calling)* Playboy murdered! Body found in *Clarion* lobby!

PETER: *(stops, astounded; to newsboy)* Here, Joe, let's have it.

NEWSBOY: *(handing paper to Peter)* Hello, Mr. Ames. Boy, I'd like to see the other guy.

PETER: There were eight of them—all equipped with brass knuckles—
The newsboy reacts to this astonishing news. Peter reads the paper.

INSERT HEADLINES:

RONNIE BELDEN FOUND IN
LOBBY OF MORNING CLARION

Knife in Chest

Aware of the *Clarion's* reputation of being first with the news, an unknown murderer or murderers tonight delivered the body of Ronnie Belden...

Medium shot—Peter and newsboy.

PETER: *(continued)* What's this?

NEWSBOY: I wouldn't know, Mr. Ames. I'm just on the distribution end.
A police siren is heard. A moment later a police car draws screeching up to the curb. A group of policemen, including Lieutenant Brent, walk over to Peter.

BRENT: *(to Peter, irascibly)* Now, look here, Pete, I never expected a double-cross from you.

PETER: I don't know a thing about it. How's the missus?

BRENT: Fine. The kids have been asking about you. *(irritated)* What's this all about? I get into headquarters and this hits me in the face.

PETER: Dunno, Mike. I wasn't in the office. I was tied up until now.
They start off into the building. A sergeant accidentally steps on Brent's heels. Brent whirls on the apologetic sergeant.

BRENT: Will you stop crawling up on me!
The sergeant makes a gesture of apology. As they start into the building.

WIPE

INTERIOR NEWSPAPER OFFICE—NIGHT
The door opens and Brent, Peter, and the policemen come striding in. The night editor gets up from his desk and hurries over to Peter.

NIGHT EDITOR: We wanted to get the papers out on the street first.

24

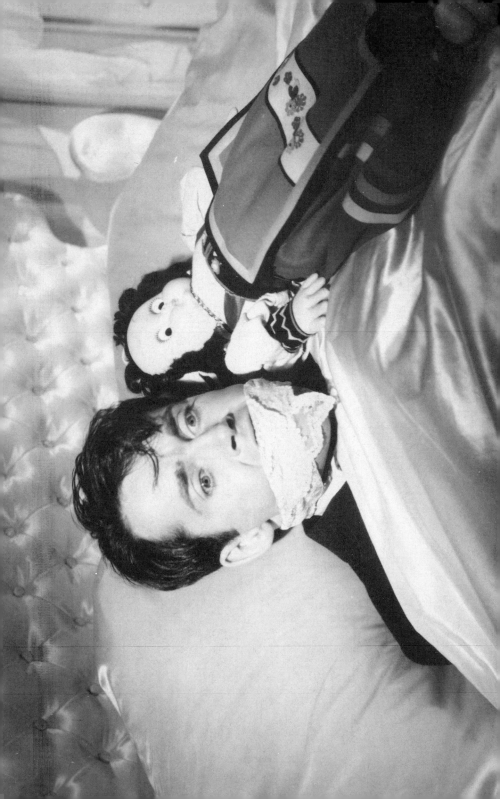

PETER: If any more bodies are found here, notify the police first.

BRENT: *(sarcastically)* If I ain't asking too much, what did you do with the body?

NIGHT EDITOR: *(to Peter)* He's in your office on the couch.

PETER: What do you want to do, haunt the couch?

Brent starts off with his officers toward Peter's office.

INTERIOR PETER'S OFFICE—NIGHT

As they enter. Police gather around body to hide it from camera.

PETER: I—er—dropped into the Lane mansion tonight—ran into Manton with a flock of her friends.

BRENT: Ran into them?—Looks like you met them head on.

PETER: I heard them say something about going over to Ronnie Belden's.

SULLIVAN: *(holding up a tooth)* He was an Elk!

BRENT: *(burns; to Sullivan)* Round up the pack of dames that run around with Manton. Bring 'em down to headquarters. Drag 'em out of bed, if you have to.

SULLIVAN: Okay—and I hope I have to!

He exits. Brent turns to Peter.

BRENT: Come on, we'll pick up Manton.

PETER: Aren't you being a little harsh, Mike? Why not wait until morning?

BRENT: Do you think I like to do this? Do you think I like to take people—men and women, human beings—and harass them, pound them, beat them, humiliate them? *(he grows excited)* But these girls, I'm going to love it!

DISSOLVE

INTERIOR BRENT'S OFFICE—HEADQUARTERS—NIGHT

The girls—still in their night attire—are seated around in a circle, surrounded by policemen. Brent stands in the middle. Peter is off at one side playing with a piece of string which he loops every once in a while into a noose. He dangles this in front of Melsa, who throughout the scene rewards him with baleful glances. The lights are on in the room and all the shades are drawn. Brent is barking at Melsa.

BRENT: Why did you take the body down to the *Clarion?*

MELSA: I thought if you read it in the paper, you'd believe it!

Brent straightens up, gets hold of himself, then turns once more to Melsa. Dora bites her nails, Helen slaps her hand.

BRENT: *(in a softened, quiet voice)* Now, Miss Manton, we've been here all night. You're tired, I'm tired, the girls are tired. All I'm asking is a simple question; which one of you girls murdered Ronnie Belden—

One of the policemen goes to the window, pulls up the shade and the morning light streams into the room. Another policeman turns off the lights.

MELSA: I've told you before, Inspector—

BRENT: *(almost in a whisper)* Lieutenant—

MELSA: I told you that the only reason we went to Ronnie Belden's apartment was because I saw Ronnie Belden come out of the Lane house. Now—are you going to let me call my lawyer?

BRENT: *(shaking his head firmly)* No!

DORA: I've got something to say.

Brent and the policemen all lean forward again.

DORA: *(continued) (brightly)* I think he committed suicide.

BRENT: *(with maniacal softness)* Yeah, you got something there. He tiptoed into the refrigerator, closed the door, and stuck the knife into himself.

He explodes and throws his arms in the air.

BRENT: *(continued)* OOOOOH!!!... *(turning to Melsa)* Look, please, won't you cooperate with us and confess?

MELSA: *(straightening up in her chair)* All right, I'll confess. I did it!

Once more the pantomime of the entire police force leaning forward.

BRENT: Why?

MELSA: Because you asked me to cooperate with you.

BRENT: *(throwing up his hands in dismay)* Look at me, a sick man. My stomach is on the blink. It's easy for me to get sick—*(exploding again)*— but I want to get sick my own way!

Peter gets up and walks over to Brent.

PETER: Wait a minute, Mike. Let me take it.

He turns to Melsa and talks quietly, sincerely.

PETER: *(continued)* Now, Miss Manton, I don't happen to agree with Lieutenant Brent. I don't think any of your girls did it, but you *are* hiding something. *(leaning forward)* Now, Melsa, why don't you tell us?

Melsa reacts at being called by her first name.

MELSA: *(coldly)* The name is Manton! You made liars and social parasites out of us. Now we girls are going to collect that million dollars from you. And as for you, Inspector Brent, false arrest is a very serious charge. You're going to finish up feeling very small and very silly without that badge to hide behind! *(turning to girls)* Who's got a lipstick?

BRENT: *(to his men, furiously)* All right, fingerprint them and put 'em in the lineup.

Policemen start pushing them out.

MELSA: *(seriously)* And all this while some homicidal maniac is loose somewhere.

An officer enters.

OFFICER: There's a lawyer here with a writ of habeas corpus for the dames.

GIRLS' AD LIBS: It's about time!

Where is he?

He was in no hurry about it!

etc.

BRENT: All right, all right. I'm going to my office to rest—*(as he walks out)*—and if those dames find another body, it'll probably be *me!*

INTERIOR BOOKING ROOM—HEADQUARTERS—DAY

Melsa's attorney is waiting. He is a very old, Union League-looking gentleman, who seemingly stands up only because he's wired. The girls start coming out through a gate into the booking room. They swarm around the attorney.

GIRLS' AD LIBS: Thank heavens, you're here, Popsie! I'm so glad to see you! *etc.*

Kit slaps him on the back. Popsie buckles, and Lee catches him just in time.

POPSIE: *(his voice quavering in protest)* Now, children, you ought to have more consideration for my age. I was fast asleep in bed, dreaming that the Grand Old Party had knocked the stuffings out of the Democrats!

Moving shot as the girls start towards the door.

MELSA: Who told you we were in jail?

POPSIE: Chap named Ames—Peter Ames.

HELEN: *(whistles two bars)* That's surprise! *(then whistling three bars)* That's light creeping in! After all, when a man calls Melsa "Melsa"...

As they walk to the door, Peter enters from the other side. Melsa looks over her shoulder at him as she walks toward the door.

KIT: Psychologists say that hate is only a few steps away from love.

MYRA: *(reflectively)* It's the lull in between that drives you crazy!

They reach the door and start out. Melsa, however, stops and looks over her shoulder once again at Peter.

MELSA: *(calling to the girls)* Wait for me downstairs, girls.

She walks over to Peter.

Close shot—Peter and Melsa.

MELSA: *(continued) (to Peter quietly)* Why did you do it?

PETER: Do what?

MELSA: Call my lawyer.

PETER: *(softly)* Maybe I'm a social climber, or a fortune hunter, or perhaps I'm beginning to like you very much ... Anyway—*(realizes he is still holding her hand)*—I realize I should let go of your hand, but the fact is I find myself not wanting to.

MELSA: *(softly)* And the fact is, I find myself wanting you not to want to let go.

PETER: *(eagerly)* Then I can see you?

MELSA: If I give you a big story—will you apologize on page one?

PETER: Make it page two and it's a deal!

MELSA: Meet me in Sheila Lane's apartment at three.

PETER: Sheila Lane?

MELSA: *(breathlessly; eager to tell her story)* Yes, I found her clip in the Lane house when I discovered the body.

Pat appears in door.

PAT: Melsa—I'm hungry!

MELSA: Good-bye—I'll be there at three.

28

DISSOLVE

EXTERIOR POLICE HEADQUARTERS—DAY
The girls are grouped on the sidewalk. Hilda is now there, and Popsie, the attorney, is standing waiting, too. A large limousine is waiting at the curb. Some girls are seated on the running board. Melsa comes out of the building.

HELEN: *(with a knowing glance inside the building)* That's one way of getting favorable publicity.

MELSA: Let's get some sleep first.

KIT: *(slapping Popsie on the back and almost knocking him down)* You can go back to the Republican administration—but don't snore.
The girls start climbing into the limousine. Brent, Peter, and a group of detectives come rushing out.

BRENT: Wait a minute! Wait a minute, you girls!

MELSA: *(impatiently)* Now what's the matter?

BRENT: You're all under arrest.
Popsie steps up.

POPSIE: Now, look here, I presented a writ of habeas corpus.
One of the cops goes to the girls who got in the car.

COP: Come on, girls, out—out!
The girls start climbing out. Brent turns to Melsa and holds out his hand.

BRENT: *(grimly)* Give me that clip!

MELSA: *(turning on Peter)* You unspeakable Judas.

PETER: Now, Melsa—

MELSA: Don't call me Melsa.

PETER: This isn't a pink tea—that knife in your door was no joke—even if I thought it was.

BRENT: What knife—

PETER: Tell you later. *(to Melsa)* This is murder—neither the police department nor I would like to get up some morning to find seven lovely debutantes murdered—After all, you look as if you had everything to live for and we propose to see that you keep on living.

POLICEMAN: You know, he makes sense to me.

BRENT: How about that clip?

MELSA: I'll give you nothing!

29

POPSIE: That's right—and don't answer any questions.

BRENT: *(rasping at Popsie)* Shut up before I run you in for obstructing justice. *(to Melsa)* Come on, give me the clip.

Melsa opens her purse, takes out the clip, and hands it to Brent.

BRENT: *(continued) (looking them over)* Withholding evidence, eh?

A homicide detail car drives up, followed by a roadster. The men get out of the car and walk up to Brent. They are carrying cameras, flashlight bulbs, and other paraphernalia.

HOMICIDE MAN: *(to Brent)* Covered Belden's apartment from stem to stern. Anything new?

BRENT: Looks like Sheila Lane done her boy friend in. We got an alarm out for her. She ducked two days ago.

PETER: How about old man Lane? If our paper knew his wife was running around with Belden, he must have known. Maybe he killed Belden and tossed his wife in the river.

BRENT: No, we checked that. Old man Lane's been out of town on business for the past week.

HOMICIDE: Say, I brought Belden's car in. *(indicating roadster)* It was standing outside his house for two days.

BRENT: *(briskly)* Okay. You and the boys catch some sleep. I'm taking these dames back to Belden's apartment—I'll make them talk if I have to keep them awake all summer.

HELEN: Now he thinks he's General Grant.

The homicide squade starts in to headquarters.

BRENT: *(to others)* Let's go. *(takes Melsa's arm)*

MELSA: Let go my arm.

POPSIE: No third degree, sir—no third degree. We're living in a democratic country. *(he stops and speaks quizzically)* Or are we?

The girls have piled into the police car leaving no room for Brent, Peter, Helen, or Melsa. Brent looks around him and notices the roadster.

BRENT: We'll use the Belden car. *(to Melsa and Helen)* You girls use the rumble seat. Ames, you drive with me.

Peter helps Helen climb into the rumble seat. Brent gets into the front seat. The top of the roadster is down. Peter starts to help Melsa climb into the rumble seat. Melsa coldly pulls away from him. As Melsa has one foot up on the car, Helen suddenly screams, and keeps screaming. Brent ducks as if he had been hit. Helen points to the bottom of the rumble seat, tries to talk but can't, succeeds only in pointing with a shaking finger at the bottom of the seat. Melsa looks down on the floor.

MELSA: *(becoming incoherent in her excitement)* That's the body— that's the body I saw in the Lane house.

Helen screams once again.

BRENT: *(to Helen)* Shut up!

Brent bends over to look. Peter bends over the rumble seat and turns the body over.

PETER: *(quietly)* It's George Lane, Sheila Lane's husband.

BRENT: *(in stupefied amazement)* Right on my own doorstep! It's contempt of court!

FADE IN

INTERIOR CORRIDOR OUTSIDE MELSA'S APARTMENT— NIGHT

Close shot of a hand ringing the door bell. Camera pulls back revealing Peter, resplendent in evening clothes, carrying a huge bouquet of flowers. The door opens and Hilda stands in the doorway.

HILDA: Oh, it's you. I told you on the phone, she won't go with you. *However, Hilda's attitude towards Peter is much more friendly than her words.*

PETER: Please, darling Hilda, I just want to talk to her.

HILDA: She says she doesn't want to talk to you. She even made me stop buying your paper... and besides, someone's coming to take her to de charity ball.

PETER: *(still persistent)* I'll force my way in.

HILDA: *(more of an apology than a threat)* If you do, she told me to throw a pitcher of water plum' in your face.

PETER: I'll risk it.

He starts to push past Hilda, who doesn't offer too much resistance.

31

INTERIOR FOYER—MELSA'S APARTMENT—NIGHT

Close shot shooting from Peter's waist up. As he steps into the foyer a sizable amount of water flies into his face.

Full shot—Hilda stands confronting a wet Peter. She holds an empty pitcher in her hand.

HILDA: *(apologetically)* It was orders—but Ah used distilled water.

Peter is drying himself with a handkerchief.

PETER: *(a quizzical note in his voice)* Do you and Melsa live this way all the time?

HILDA: Well, Ah've done mah best. She's in the living room. But I warn you—you-all better not go in dere. She's in a nasty mood—and when Ah says nasty, Ah ain't mincin' words!

Melsa appears at the doorway.

MELSA: *(to Hilda, coldly)* I thought I told you to keep him out.

Peter's manner becomes a trifle abject.

PETER: Melsa, please—*(taking a newspaper from his pocket)* Look, I apologized publicly. I humiliated myself. Can't you forgive me? *(sincerely)* I never ran after a woman before—that is, I never admitted it—but I'm running after you now.

MELSA: *(unimpressed, coldly)* You're on a treadmill, Mr. Ames. You may keep on running, but you'll remain in the same spot.

PETER: *(turning to Hilda, plaintively)* Hilda, for Pete's sakes, will you get out of here? I've got things to say, and I can't say them with you standing there staring at me!

MELSA: *(sharply)* Hilda, you stay where you are.

HILDA: *(with a look at Melsa)* You don't know what's good for you!

She exits. Melsa turns to go back to the living room. Peter grabs her by the shoulder and turns her around.

PETER: *(earnestly)* You stand here and listen! Before I knew you, I disliked you intensely. When I met you I disliked you—intensely. Even now I dislike you intensely—that is, the sensible, sane portion of me. You neither spin nor do you sew; you're just a decorative, useless member of a rapidly vanishing class. *(with a change of voice)* But there's an insane side of me that becomes a little violent every time I think of you!

MELSA: *(still unimpressed)* Getting rid of a million-dollar suit wouldn't have anything to do with your change in affection, would it?

PETER: *(looking her over contemptuously)* You *are* a nasty creature, but in time I'll beat it out of you. I know why you're going to the ball. I also know that Sheila Lane is chairwoman of the Entertainment Committee and hasn't missed one of these affairs in five years and she might show up. So, you see, I'm going for the same reason you are.

MELSA: *I'm* going because I'm charitably inclined—

PETER: Well, if that's your mood, come with me and I'll let you pay the cab fare.

The door opens and a young man typically Melsa's class enters.

MELSA: Hello, Harold. I'll be ready in a moment.

She goes to the closet, opens it, and looks around for her cape. The two men stand looking at each other, neither one quite sure whether he should start introducing himself. Melsa comes out of the closet, a cape around her shoulders. She takes Harold's arm and starts for the door. Harold, with a quizzical look at Peter, waits to be introduced, but Melsa ignores the situation. As Harold and Melsa start out of the door, Peter calls after them.

PETER: Very glad to have met you, Harold. Drop in some day, and we'll have another heart-to-heart talk.

Harold is startled, confused, and embarrassed.

HAROLD: *(unhappily)* Ah—oh, yes—sure.

Melsa and Harold exit. Peter stands looking after them, as we

DISSOLVE OUT

DISSOLVE IN

INTERIOR COUNTRY CLUB FOYER—NIGHT

People in evening dress are standing around conversing, smiling, etc. Peter enters, leaves his hat and coat at the checking counter. Brent, dressed in full evening regalia, enters scene and goes over to Peter. Peter looks him over amusedly.

PETER: Well, I never thought I'd live to see the day you'd turn your back on the middle class.

BRENT: *(looking at his clothes in disgust)* Look at it! And in the expense account, they call it a disguise!

PETER: *(eyeing Brent closely)* Having a good time?

33

BRENT: You know why I'm here, and I know why you're here.

PETER: There are no ulterior motives in my charitable impulses.

BRENT: Yeah—I'd like to grab Sheila Lane, too.

A reporter enters and goes over to Peter.

REPORTER: Hey, boss, I found out about that—

He sees Brent and stops.

PETER: *(nodding at Brent)* He's okay.

REPORTER: It was a tough job, but I dug it up—covered every insurance company—

Melsa enters from the ladies' lounge, looks at them, and stays in the background.

REPORTER: *(continued)* George Lane left an insurance policy of $250,000.

BRENT: Why didn't you come to me—I could have saved you the job—we knew that.

PETER: *(turning to Brent)* Well, it's possible a wife would kill a husband for that amount of money. You might even call it justifiable homicide.

BRENT: The wife isn't the beneficiary. It's his partner, Thomas.

Melsa saunters nearby. She lights a cigarette and pretends not to notice them. Brent and Peter look at each other significantly.

PETER: *(turning to reporter)* Thanks a lot, Jim. See you at the office.

Peter takes Brent's arm and they walk out of the room. Melsa looks after them, then follows.

INTERIOR COUNTRY CLUB CORRIDOR—NIGHT

Trucking shot. Melsa comes out of the foyer and walks down the corridor. Brent and Peter are standing there whispering. When they see her, they walk again along the corridor. She turns and follows them. They go through a swinging door. As Melsa reaches the door it swings closed, revealing a sign on it saying "MEN'S LOUNGE." The door swings open again, and a man stands in the doorway face to face with Melsa. Melsa, without stopping her stride, turns and walks away.

INTERIOR MEN'S LOUNGE—NIGHT

Medium shot—in the washroom. Brent and Peter are standing over adjoining wash basins washing their hands.

BRENT: *(shaking his head dubiously)* It don't make sense to me. Thomas has got ten million dollars in the bank. Why would he kill his partner for two hundred and fifty thousand?

PETER: *(drying his hands on a towel)* What makes you sure he's got ten million dollars in the bank?

BRENT: That guy's as solid as the Bank of England. He's got relatives all through the banking business.

PETER: Why don't you subpoena his books and find out?

BRENT: Listen, ain't I got enough with Manton trying to get my badge? Do I have to get Wall Street on my neck, too?

A detective in evening clothes enters.

BRENT: *(continued) (turning to him)* Any sign of Sheila Lane?

DETECTIVE: No.

BRENT: *(to Peter)* How I wish I could get my hands on that dame.

PETER: *(slyly reproving)* And you a married man, Lieutenant!

INTERIOR BALLROOM— NIGHT

Couples are dancing, etc. Dora is sitting by the wall, a forlorn, lonesome creature. She has the vague, blank stare of the wallflower who pretends she is waiting for someone. A man walks past. Dora brightens. The man, unseeing, walks past her. The smile fades on Dora's lips. She relaxes again. Another unescorted male walks up. Dora's smile is less hopeful. The man barely nods at her and walks past. Peter enters scene and walks over to Dora.

PETER: Can I buy you a drink?

Dora looks behind her to see if he's talking to someone else.

DORA: Who, me?

PETER: Of course.

DORA: *(dazed by her good fortune)* Gee whiz—Could I take your arm?

Peter offers his arm with a smile. They walk off.

INTERIOR BAR—NIGHT

People are standing, sitting, and lounging against the bar in various positions and stages of alcohol. Dora and Peter come into scene. Dora climbs up on a stool.

DORA: *(to Peter)* Can I get anything I want?

PETER: Haven't you been getting what you want?

DORA: Oh no. My father keeps an eagle eye on me. He says I'm the old-fashioned-girl type.
PETER: Are you?
DORA: Well—never after midnight. *(turning to bartender; bravely)* Straight rye.
PETER: *(to bartender)* Bourbon.
    He turns to Dora.

INTERIOR BALLROOM—DANCE FLOOR—NIGHT
Melsa is dancing by. Over her partner's shoulder, she eyes Peter and Dora curiously.

INTERIOR BAR—NIGHT
    Peter puts down his drink and leans confidentially toward Dora.
PETER: Look, would you do something for me?
DORA: *(her eyes opening wide)* Gee whiz!
PETER: I'm thinking of investing with Alan Thomas. I've heard a rumor he's been losing money. I haven't much money—it's my life savings—and you wouldn't want me to risk it, would you?
DORA: Oh, no... but if you ever need money—my grandpa left me some... I wouldn't need much collateral.
PETER: I couldn't think of it—Your father is on the Exchange Board; maybe you could ask him about Thomas. He'd know.
DORA: Gee whiz!—Yes.
    She gets off the stool and almost goes to her knees from the effect of one drink. She starts to weave, stops, turns:
DORA: *(continued)* Have you enough to pay for the drink?
PETER: I can make it.
    She continues to weave through the crowd, finally gets hold of herself, and starts walking firmly.
    Camera follows her until she reaches a group of important-looking men. She walks over to one of them and addresses him.
DORA: Oh, Dad!
    Mr. Fenton turns to his daughter.
FENTON: Yes, dear.
    He takes her arm and they walk a short distance away from the group.

DORA: Is it true Mr. Thomas, Mr. Lane's partner, lost a lot of money in the market?

FENTON: It's none of your business.

DORA: But I'm your daughter—

FENTON: It's still none of your business.

DORA: *(desperately)* You don't know what this means to me—I must know—it's life or death—Is Mr. Thomas about to go busted, Daddy?

A man and woman passing, turn suddenly.

THOMAS: *(startled)* Who's been talking about me? I've had no losses. I'm solvent. I'm—*(to Fenton)* Fenton, have you been talking!

FENTON: *(soothingly)* If I were you, Thomas...

THOMAS: I'll report you to the board, Fenton.

WOMAN: *(to Thomas)* You're behaving like a guilty man.

DORA: Excuse me!

She ducks away from them, leaving Thomas looking after her with a puzzled, frightened frown. Melsa walks over to Dora, puts her arm around her affectionately.

MELSA: *(a glint in her eye)* Hello, dear, enjoying yourself?

DORA: *(infinite pity in her voice)* Oh, Melsa, your poor friend. He's going to invest his life's savings with Mr. Thomas. He asked me to ask Dad whether Mr. Thomas lost a lot of money in the market.

MELSA: *(reflectively)* Oh, he did, did he?

DORA: I don't know. Dad wouldn't tell me.

Melsa thinks a moment, then makes up her mind.

MELSA: Now, dear, you run along to Mr. Ames, and tell him I just learned that his newspaper office is on fire.

DORA: *(shocked)* It is? Oh, poor Mr. Ames—his life's savings, and now his newspaper office burns down!

Melsa turns and hurries away. Camera follows her as she goes through the door. Coming from the opposite direction is Helen. Melsa grabs hold of Helen and turns her around.

MELSA: Come on, we've got work to do!

HELEN: But I've got a date in the garden.

MELSA: Send Pat out there—it'll teach him a lesson!

She pulls Helen along.

Medium shot—at bar. As Dora runs in to Peter.

DORA: *(excitedly)* Oh, Mr. Ames—your newspaper is on fire—

37

PETER: What!

He jumps off his chair and starts for door, stops after a few steps, and turns.

PETER: *(continued)* How do you know?

DORA: Melsa told me.

PETER: *(quietly)* Oh, she did—*(to bartender)* Another rye for the lady—*(he tosses a bill on counter)* Miss Manton has just lit a fire at which she's going to burn her dainty little fingers.

Camera follows as he goes toward door—at door it swings toward Thomas and woman who are behind some palms.

THOMAS: *(excitedly)* You can't leave me—

WOMAN: Why not be honest?

THOMAS: *You* couldn't be.

WOMAN: *(with a smile)* Strangely enough this time I am—I'm a rather expensive possession.

THOMAS: What they're whispering isn't true!

WOMAN: *(disregarding his outburst)* Why don't you go in for something a little cheaper?

THOMAS: I have a quarter of a million coming to me.

WOMAN: The insurance policy.

THOMAS: How did *you* know?

WOMAN: *(with a smile)* Your partner told me—before he conveniently died. Tell me, did you kill him?

THOMAS: I didn't—

WOMAN: Where were you that night?

THOMAS: Walking, walking alone—trying to decide whether to kill you or marry you.

WOMAN: I'm sure either one would be just as deadly. *(she walks off)*

DISSOLVE OUT

DISSOLVE IN

INTERIOR OFFICE BUILDING CORRIDOR—NIGHT
Medium shot shooting down corridor. Around the bend come Melsa and Helen. Helen is carrying a kit of automobile tools. They stop at a door marked "LANE & THOMAS, BROKERS, STOCK EX-

CHANGE." *Melsa tries the door. It doesn't give. She pulls at it quietly but it remains locked. Melsa turns to Helen.*

MELSA: Give me the tools.

Helen, in handing over the kit, trips; and the kit falls to the floor, making a terrific clatter.

MELSA: *(continued)* Ssssh!

She bends down and as she picks up the kit more tools drop out, adding to the clatter.

HELEN: Ssssh!

Melsa takes a chisel out of the kit and puts the chisel into the jamb of the door and tugs at it. Helen puts her arm around Melsa and tugs, too. The door resists for a while, then suddenly flies open. The glass pane in the door shatters, making a terrific racket. The girls stand petrified for a moment, look around up and down the corridor until they are sure no one is coming, then turn on their flashlights and walk in.

INTERIOR OUTER OFFICE—NIGHT

The girls enter, look around for a moment, then cross to a door leading to the inner office.

INTERIOR INNER OFFICE—NIGHT

The girls enter and search around with their flashlights. One of the flashlights centers on a metal file. They walk over. They try to open the files, but the file drawers are locked. Helen tugs at the drawers. Melsa takes the chisel and puts it in the lock on top of the files and pries at it.

MELSA: *(as she tugs at the lock)* And I always thought it was so difficult to be a crook. Why, all you need is a chisel!

HELEN: Let's not look on it as a permanent occupation.

The lock breaks open and the file opens. Suddenly the lights in the room are switched on. The girls jump up and look around. Peter is standing behind them. A young, scholarly looking fellow in thick glasses is standing next to him. They are standing by the safe. Peter smiles at the girls.

PETER: Thank you very much, girls. It's very sweet of you.

MELSA: *(frowning at him)* When did you get in here?

39

PETER: We were here when you girls gently stole in. By the way, there's nothing in the file.

HELEN: *(looking relieved)* I, for one, am glad you're here.

MELSA: *(to Helen, with a scornful look)* Mrs. Benedict Arnold! *(whirling on Peter)* And you—you needn't look so complacent. I wouldn't be so proud of duping a naive, trusting girl like Dora—asking her to sneak around—pick up information—do your dirty errands for you!

PETER: *(not the least taken aback)* Well, you took advantage of her, too.

MELSA: That's different. She's a friend of mine. She's nothing to you.

PETER: Still we're all here for the same purpose. *(nodding to the young man)* I brought up an expert in safes, Mr.—

SAFECRACKER: *(quickly)* No names, boss, no names!

HELEN: *(gazing at him in awe)* Are you a real crook?

SAFECRACKER: The last lawyer who defended me said I was antisocial. I kinda like that better than crook.

PETER: *(indicating safe)* All right, Mr. X. Let's go to work.

SAFECRACKER: Naw, not in front of witnesses.

PETER: *(indicating Melsa)* She's all right; she's the girl I'm going to marry. You know, a wife can't testify against her husband.

SAFECRACKER: Yeah, but she could testify against me.

MELSA: *(with a cold look at Peter, addresses the safecracker)* I could marry you. As a matter of fact, I'd prefer it.

> *Peter, standing behind the safecracker, pantomimes to Melsa to let Mr. X go to work.*

SAFECRACKER: Looks like she isn't going to marry you.

> *Peter signals to Melsa to say "yes."*

MELSA: Why, yes, of course, I'm going to marry him.

SAFECRACKER: *(nodding at Helen)* How about this other dame?

HELEN: I'm going to be his second wife.

> *Peter reaches into his pocket and takes out some bills.*

PETER: I'm raising the ante fifty bucks.

> *The safecracker looks at the bills, then at the safe. He takes the $50.00 from Peter. Opening his bag, he takes out a delicate stethoscope, puts it over his ears, and bends down in front of the safe, as we*

DISSOLVE

INTERIOR INNER OFFICE—NIGHT
Medium shot shooting to safe. Mr. X swings the safe door open, takes out some ledgers, and hands them over to Peter.
PETER: *(opening ledgers)* All right, Mr. X, if you'll get your photostatic machine ready.
Peter turns to girls who stand by waiting.
PETER: This'll take a little time, girls.
HELEN: That's all right. We'll start planning Melsa's trousseau.
Melsa gives Helen a dirty look, then walks over to the safe, rummages around a bit, and takes out a packet and looks at it.

INSERT THE PACKET
Marked: GEORGE LANE—Personal
Back to scene: Melsa hurriedly hides the packet behind her back.
PETER: *(referring to trousseau)* Lay off pale salmon, I hate it!
MR. X: Here's a certified profit-and-loss statement, Mr. Ames. Looks like you were right.
Ames takes the sheet. Helen and Melsa try to see over his shoulder. He folds the paper tantalizingly and puts it into his pocket.
HELEN: I can't believe he did it!
PETER: I like loyalty in a woman—and *hate* deceit. *(barking at Melsa)* Give me that envelope!
MELSA: *(refusing to give it up)* It says "personal"—it's none of your business. Anyway, this is Lane's paper and you're investigating Thomas.
Peter snatches the envelope out of Melsa's hand and opens it. Melsa and Helen peer over his shoulder as he takes out some papers and looks them over. He opens a passbook.
PETER: One thousand withdrawn the 8th—a thousand the 15th—one the 22nd—looks like a thousand every week—and here's twenty thousand withdrawn the day Lane was murdered. Mr. X, what does it smell like to you?
MR. X: *(wisely)* Blackmail!
Peter opens some more papers.
PETER: *(with a surprised whistle)* Well, Mr. Lane knew everything about his wife! Looks very much as if Sheila had a very interesting and

41

crowded career—as far as men are concerned. *(looking through papers)* Here's some dope on Ronnie. *(whistles)* Here's something interesting. Maybe this is what cost him the twenty grand. Sheila was married to a convict named Norris before she married Lane. He's doing a ten-year stretch right now. Here are the clippings on him. *(holds up the papers)*

INSERT OF A PICTURE
Showing a man handcuffed to a detective. The caption reads:

No. 3572, Eddie Norris, starting for a ten-year term at Joliet.

There is another picture—of Sheila Lane, and the caption reads:

Mrs. Eddie Norris.

BACK TO SCENE
MELSA: *(reflectively)* So Sheila was married to number three-five-seven-two.
Suddenly a voice behind them says, in a quiet, menacing tone:
VOICE (NORRIS): Am I being paged?
They all whirl around, and there standing before them is the man whose picture we had seen in the newspaper clipping. He is now middle-aged. He doesn't look like the usual convict type (Porter Hall might be the type). Norris has a pistol in each hand pointed at the group. Peter, trying to calm the girls, pretends an ease he doesn't feel.
PETER: Hello, Eddie. Thought you were in jail.
NORRIS: Got out a week ago. They knocked off a couple of years because I was a good boy.
The safecracker takes a step towards Norris.
SAFECRACKER: *(pleadingly)* Now, look, Eddie, I had nothing to do with this. I'm just up here on a job. Got a hundred smackers for it.
NORRIS: *(tonelessly)* Shut up, rat! *(turning to Peter)* Put those papers back in the envelope.
PETER: *(complying)* You know, Eddie, you've just done a stretch, and if they nab you with those water pistols, you're going to catch an awful spanking.
NORRIS: *(still in the same dull, monotonous tone)* Toss it over.

42

Peter flips the envelope right at Norris. It hits Norris in the eyes. As he puts his hands up to his eyes, Peter dives at his legs and tackles him. The guns go off. Melsa, startled, falls over, her head striking the lead of the couch. She lies there motionless. Helen rushes over to Melsa. Peter and Norris are struggling on the floor. Mr. X runs over, brings the chisel down on Norris's head. Norris lies still. Peter gets up, starts to straighten his clothes and brush himself off.

PETER: *(to Mr. X)* Thanks.

SAFECRACKER: That'll cost you another fifty bucks.

Helen is still bending over Melsa.

HELEN: She's dead! She's dead! He shot her! Melsa, talk to me!

Peter runs over, bends down, and takes Melsa in his arms.

PETER: Melsa, darling, please—please don't be dead!

Peter puts her head on his chest.

PETER: *(continued)* She's alive. Rub her wrists. I'll get some water.

He gets up and hurries into the other room. Helen bends over Melsa and starts rubbing her wrists. Peter comes hurrying in, carrying a glass of water. He bends down and throws the water in Melsa's face. She comes to, sputtering.

PETER: *(continued)* Don't worry—it's distilled water.

MELSA: *(indignantly)* What do you mean by calling me darling?

DISSOLVE

INTERIOR MELSA'S LIVING ROOM—DAY

Melsa, in a dressing gown, is lying on her face on a sofa. Hilda is putting cold compresses on the back of her head. Melsa sniffles and groans.

MELSA: Are you sure there's no hole there, Hilda? It feels empty.

HILDA: *(frowning)* It don' only feel empty—it *is* empty! If it wahn't, you'all wouldn't be mixin' into things lak dis!

MELSA: *(her voice very tired)* Hilda, you're fired. Please pack your bags and go and leave me here to die alone. *(she sneezes, then groans)* Oh, my poor head.

Suddenly our girls barge in excitedly, newspapers in their hands. Hilda looks at them and then walks out with a wry look. The girls scatter around. Myra at once goes to the telephone. Pat walks over to a candy dish and starts nibbling.

LEE: Hilda!

MELSA: Girls! Please, my head!

KIT: Why didn't you take us last night? We missed all the fun—

MELSA: What's funny about a bump on the head.

PAT: I think it's beautiful getting wounded in the line of duty.

KIT: *(ecstatic)* Imagine capturing a murderer!

HELEN: Well, he claims an alibi. *(reading from newspaper)* "Edward Norris, held on suspicion of the murders of George Lane, Ronnie Belden, and Sheila Lane, whose body has not yet been found, claims an alibi—declares he was with girl friend, Frances Glesk, at hockey match at time of George Lane's murder. So far, attempts of police to locate Miss Glesk have proved fruitless."

Front doorbell rings.

MELSA: *(contemptuously)* The police—all they know is to blow a whistle and tie up traffic.

HILDA'S VOICE: You-all cain't go in dere.

WOMAN'S VOICE: Oh, yes I can. Get out of my way!

An attractive Broadway-type woman forces her way past Hilda into the room. She is a trifle on the loud side and at the moment is in an obviously hysterical mood. Hilda has hold of the woman by the arm.

WOMAN: *(continued)* It's all your fault! If you hadn't been there, he wouldn't have been nabbed. And all he wanted was the papers. Now they've tied him up with the killings—

Pat stares at the woman, her mouth open, and a sardine in her hand suspended in mid-air.

WOMAN: *(continued)* Why should he want to bump Lane off? Why should he want to kill Belden? Sheila Lane doesn't mean a thing to him. Sure he was married to her—but he loves me—he loves me!

Suddenly her eyes roll up and she falls to the floor in a faint.

MYRA: Gee, how he must love her!

Myra hangs up the phone and starts over to the woman. Melsa and the girls rush over to the woman and carry her over to the couch. As they carry her, the girls ad lib:

AD LIBS: Get some water!

44

Take her shoes off!

What's her shoes got to do with it?

Aren't you supposed to loosen something or other?

One of the girls comes over with a glass of water. They sprinkle the woman's face with it, then force some down her throat. Slowly the woman comes to, her eyes open and she looks around.

WOMAN: What did I do—pass out?

MELSA: I'm afraid you did.

PAT: I bet she's hungry.

HELEN: *(to Pat)* Listen, if you're looking for more food, you faint for it yourself!

MELSA: You're Frances Glesk, aren't you?

The woman nods, then speaks in a weak voice.

GLESK: I'm sorry to bother you, but you're a woman—I'm appealing to you. I must have some money to get out of town. I've been ducking the police for two days.

MELSA: You're Eddie Norris's alibi. If you were with him at the hockey game, why don't you go to the police?

GLESK: Because—because—*(the words catch in her throat)* I—I—

The tears start in her eyes. She begins to weep softly.

GLESK: *(continued)*—Because the kind of alibi I could give him would send him to the chair—he wasn't with me all the time—between hockey periods he went out for a smoke—but he didn't do it! He didn't do it! He's not that kind.

HELEN: I suppose those two guns he pointed at us down in Lane's office were papier-mâché!

GLESK: I could go to the police but I'd have to lie. I'm a two-time loser. If they catch me at it, it'll be perjury—that would mean a long stretch for me.

HELEN: You're an unselfish sort of a gal, aren't you?*(suspiciously)* You didn't happen to know George Lane?

GLESK: Only slightly.

MELSA: *(to Myra)* What are you driving at?

MYRA: It strikes me that all this rigamarole makes out a perfect alibi for herself.

MELSA: We all knew George Lane, but we didn't kill him either.

Hilda starts. The doorbell rings. Hilda exits.

MELSA: *(continued)* I believe you. And we'll help you. *(to girls)* We've got work to do.

> *We hear Peter's voice outside in the foyer.*

PETER'S VOICE: Hello, Hilda. Is Miss Manton in?

HILDA'S VOICE: No, she ain't. She done left for South America.

> *Melsa whispers to Frances Glesk.*

MELSA: You just sit tight. Don't do any talking—you're Dora's cousin from Chattanooga.

> *Peter enters, a long thin box in one hand, and a basket of fruit, candy, and champagne bottles in his other arm.*

PETER: Hello, girls—came up to celebrate. Got a twenty-five dollar raise. They offered me the money or new furniture in the office. I took the money.

MELSA: A raise for what?

PETER: *(beginning to open champagne bottle)* Oh, catching a murderer—

MELSA: Wasn't that a little premature of your employers? Norris hasn't been convicted yet.

PETER: He's unquestionably guilty. He goes before the grand jury in an hour. *(he looks at Glesk curiously)*

MELSA: Oh, Peter, this is Dora's cousin, Ann Spaulding, from Chattanooga.

PETER: *(smiles at Frances Glesk)* How do you do?

> *Glesk nods.*

PETER: *(continued)* Welcome to the gang—where'd you say you came from?

MELSA: *(quickly)* Chattanooga.

PETER: Get the exact address. We'll send her an invitation to our marriage.

MELSA: Marriage?

> *The girls look at each other in astonishment.*

PETER: Well, Helen witnessed your promise last night.

GIRLS' AD LIBS: Oh, Melsa!

Why didn't you tell?

Married!

When did you decide?

How long has this been going on?

MYRA: *(very softly)* Congratulations, Peter. May I be the first?

> She puts her arms around Peter and kisses him long and
> emphatically. Melsa gives Myra a long feminine look which has a
> certain percentage of jealousy in it.

MELSA: Why should I marry him? If I want to marry a fortune hunter, I
can go to Europe and marry a professional fortune hunter.

> Peter takes out a bottle of champagne from the basket and starts to
> open it.

PETER: *(to Melsa, over his shoulder)* Listen, I'm determined to make
you happy if I have to drag your name through the breach of promise
courts to do it. *(turning to Frances Glesk)* You're from Chattanooga,
where they have a higher sense of values. Don't you think I'm a good
catch?

GLESK: I don't know.

PETER: You must know the Carlisles—? They're an old family—mint
julep and all that...

MELSA: *(quickly)* Let's have a drink.

> Some of the girls get glasses and Peter starts pouring out drinks.

PETER: I'll have to develop a taste for this stuff. Since we're going to be
married and you've got plenty of money, we can afford it. *(handing a
glass to Melsa)*

> Peter turns to Frances Glesk.

PETER: *(continued)* Aren't you drinking, Miss Spaulding?

> Glesk reaches for glass.

MELSA: *(hurriedly)* Er—she never touches the stuff. *(an authoritative
note in her voice)* Well, thanks for dropping in.

> Myra steps up to Peter and takes his arm.

MYRA: I'll walk you down to the elevator.

> Dora enters in street clothes.

PETER: *(severely to Dora)* Where've you been? Melsa and I've just been
engaged and you haven't been here. Say, I like your cousin—even if she
won't hoist a mug with us.

DORA: *(in surprise)* My cousin.

MELSA: *(quickly)* From Chattanooga—she just got in.

DORA: But...

MELSA: *(indicating Glesk)* You *are* surprised to see her, aren't you,
dear—Now go kiss her hello.

DORA: But, she ain't...
  Helen kicks her.
HELEN: Now go kiss her hello—don't let a little family quarrel stand in the way—
  Dora goes to Glesk, kisses her.
DORA: *(bewildered)* Hello—
PETER: Well—good-bye. *(starts for door.)*
  Girls give sigh of relief. Peter stops.
PETER: *(continued)* Oh, may I use your phone?
  Peter goes over to the phone and dials a number. The girls all watch him.
PETER: *(continued) (at phone)* Hello...Hello...Lieutenant Brent.
  Pat stops playing the piano. There is silence in the room. Frances Glesk looks intently at Peter.
PETER: *(continued)* Hello—Brent? You looking for Norris's girl friend, Frances Glesk? Well, she's up here in Melsa Manton's apartment. Come and get her. *(turns to Dora)* If I were you, I'd use a little more discrimination in the choice of my relatives!
  Melsa picks up a champagne bottle and lifts it to throw at Peter. Helen stops her. Melsa puts it down, but keeps on glaring at Peter.

DISSOLVE OUT

DISSOLVE IN

EXTERIOR MADISON SQUARE GARDEN—NIGHT
Close shot of newspaper headline:

NORRIS ALIBI SHATTERED

Camera pulls back to reveal Melsa and the girls standing in front of Madison Square Garden. The girls are grouped around a car. Lee is resting against a bicycle. In the shot we see that a subway is being excavated. Melsa puts the paper down and speaks to the girls.
MELSA: *(seriously)* This isn't play any longer. We're dealing with a man's life. The rest period in hockey games is ten minutes.
  Melsa looks at her wristwatch.

48

MELSA: *(continued)* It's up to us to prove whether Norris could or could not get up to the Lane house, kill a man, and get back in that time. I'm purposely making it the same time of night because then we'll be facing the same traffic problems. Helen, you take a cab. Myra, you take the bus; and Kit, the subway. Pat, walk as fast as you can—and don't stop at restaurants. All right, start off.

Helen starts hailing a cab. Lee starts off on her bike. The others go down the street. The rest of the girls remain with Melsa.

DISSOLVE OUT

DISSOLVE IN

INTERIOR STAR NEWSPAPER OFFICE—DAY (PROCESS BACKGROUND)
Close shot of proof sheet of the New York Star. *The lead is:*

NORRIS ALIBI SUBSTANTIATED

The subhead is:

Series of Tests
by Miss Melsa Manton
Prove Norris's Presence at
Scene of Crime Impossible.

Camera pulls back revealing the editor's office. Through the closed door we see (process background) the usual newspaper office activity. On the glass door is printed: NEW YORK STAR, Editor's Office. *The editor is a rather elderly, pompous gentleman who at the moment is addressing Melsa, seated across the desk from him.*

MELSA: *(reading)* "While with their usual enthusiasm the police were browbeating an innocent man, Melsa Manton and her group of public-spirited friends have unearthed a witness who substantiated Ed Norris's alibi . . . " *(looks up at the editor)*

EDITOR: We're grateful for the opportunity to hammer the police a bit.

MELSA: *(getting up)* You'll keep this headline off the streets for twenty minutes, as you promised—

49

EDITOR: We're old-fashioned enough to keep our word.

MELSA: *(starts off, clutching paper)* I'm going down to the district attorney's. They're going to indict Norris.

EDITOR: It's just like the police to fasten on a scapegoat. *(calls after her)* Miss Manton, any time you want a job as a reporter, come to me.

DISSOLVE

INTERIOR DISTRICT ATTORNEY'S OUTER OFFICE—DAY

A secretary is seated at the desk. The door opens and a very testy-looking individual (Clarence Wilson) enters and walks over to the male secretary.

ATTORNEY: Is the D.A. in?

The secretary starts to answer.

ATTORNEY: *(continued)* No, he ain't. He's never in to me. Where's my client? He's not at headquarters. He's not at the Tombs. He's *got* to be here! I demand to see my client!

SECRETARY: And who *is* your client?

ATTORNEY: *(snapping at him)* You know well enough who my client is! You'd know if I was a member of your boss's club! But I've got my rights, here, the same as any criminal—I—*(corrects himself)*—that is, I mean criminal lawyer—

SECRETARY: *(annoyed)* Now see here, Mr. Counselor, just tell me—quietly tell me—who is your client and who are you?

ATTORNEY: Edward Norris is my client. He ain't at headquarters and he ain't here. What have you done with him? If you're giving him a third degree—

SECRETARY: *(annoyed)* We don't give the third degree here, sir—

ATTORNEY: *(nastily)* Oh, so you don't give it here—you give it down at headquarters—you've beaten him up, he's in the hospital—Come on, what is it!

SECRETARY: *(backing up)* I refuse to answer—you can't intimidate me—and anyway, please sit down and wait your turn...

The door opens and Norris comes in handcuffed to two detectives. Brent and Peter, who shows the effects of a terrible hangover, enter accompanied by a few more detectives.

50

ATTORNEY: There he is!

He starts over to Norris. Brent steps in front of Norris and pushes the attorney aside.

BRENT: All right, Gabby, sit down. We'll get to you, later.

ATTORNEY: I demand to speak to my client. I stand on my constitutional rights.

BRENT: *(unimpressed)* You sit on your constitutional rights for a few minutes.

Brent and the detectives exit into the D.A.'s office.

ATTORNEY: *(calling through door)* Norris, don't say a word!

The door slams in his face. He strides towards the outer door.

ATTORNEY: *(continued) (grumbling angrily)* I'll be back with a habeas corpus.

As he opens the door to go out he finds himself face to face with Melsa.

ATTORNEY: *(continued)* And if they hurt one hair of Norris's head in there—you'd better find a hole to crawl into...

Melsa walks past him and goes over to the secretary's desk.

MELSA: *(to secretary)* I'd like to speak to the district attorney, please.

SECRETARY: *(toughly)* He's busy.

MELSA: Mr. Ames and Mr. Brent don't happen to be in there, too?

SECRETARY: I refuse to answer.

MELSA: I must see the district attorney immediately.

SECRETARY: *(rising wrathfully)* I'll not be intimidated—sit down and wait your turn.

There is a buzz on the Dictaphone behind secretary. He jumps nervously. He goes back, flips up key.

SECRETARY: *(continued)* Yes, sir!

VOICE: (over Dictaphone) Bring in that police report.

SECRETARY: Yes, sir!

He picks up a report from his desk and goes to door, opens it.

D.A.'S VOICE: *(through open door)* Now, Norris, we're going before the grand jury in a few minutes—why don't you write out a confession and save us a lot of trouble?

The door closes. Melsa walks impatiently up and down. Door opens again.

BRENT'S VOICE: We checked with the warden at Sing Sing—you swore you'd kill anybody who mistreated Sheila—Old man Lane was known to have...

Secretary enters and closes door.

MELSA: *(to secretary)* I must see the district attorney at once—

SECRETARY: *(tapping the top of his desk with his fingers—trying to control himself)* Indeed! Young lady, the rule of this office is that you wait your turn.

Melsa starts for door marked "PRIVATE." Secretary hurriedly gets in her way; he speaks excitedly...

SECRETARY: *(continued)* Where are you going! You can't go in there! It's against the law—and anyway you must wait your turn.

The buzzer sounds again. Keeping one hand on the door knob, he reaches over and flips up key—he speaks sharply.

SECRETARY: *(continued)* Yes!

D.A.'S VOICE: What's that?

SECRETARY: *(voice softening)* I beg your pardon.

D.A.'S VOICE: Bring in that file on Norris.

SECRETARY: Yes, sir!

With a "look what you've done now" look on his face he goes to the file, turning his back. As he digs in file, Melsa removes large pin from flowers, pins newspaper to tail of secretary's coat. He goes to door with file, opens it to enter.

NORRIS'S VOICE: Why should I kill anybody?—I've got a good job now—foreman on the new subway.

INTERIOR OFFICE—DAY

As secretary enters with file and crosses to desk.

NORRIS: I said I was going straight and I am.

PETER: *(his voice showing the effects of the drinks)* It's just a matter of evidence. Now, Norris, you know a jury of twelve men good and true will find you guilty. You're known to have hated Lane, and you were willing to murder me and some very lovely girls—to destroy evidence.

As secretary starts for door, there is a silence in room. The others have seen paper. Their eyes widen. Suddenly Brent makes a leap for the secretary's coattail, followed by the others. As Brent snatches the paper off the coattail the secretary leaps sky high.

SECRETARY: *(affronted)* Sir!

52

BRENT: Where did you get this?

SECRETARY: I didn't do anything—

D.A.: Where did you get this, you fool!

SECRETARY: You assured me, sir, this position was one of dignity and decorum!

PETER: Will you answer their questions—oh, my head.

SECRETARY: Well, there's a young lady outside...

Brent flings him out of the way—they all dash for the door.

INTERIOR DISTRICT ATTORNEY'S OUTER OFFICE—DAY

As they all rush in.

D.A.: *(sternly)* See here, young lady, I can't allow you to do this to my office.

MELSA: Here are the affidavits—the legal proof that the law of physics is maintained—one object cannot be in two places at the same time!

PETER: *(in a hurt tone)* Another paper prints it! You know it might cost me my job.

MELSA: *(unaffected)* That's all right, my dear—I'll use my influence to get you on the W.P.A.

BRENT: *(controlling himself)* And all my life I wanted to be a cop.

MELSA: I suppose I should have left you alone. You had a very lovely suspect and you probably could have proven, in your inimitable way, that he did it. The fact that he's innocent would never disturb your sleep. You had a case—you'd bring it to a satisfactory conclusion. A man would die for it, and the real murderer would go free, as long as Inspector Brent kept his badge! Which, by the bye, he won't keep anyway if we can help it.

Melsa turns and walks out. They stand looking after her.

PETER: Isn't she wonderful? That's the girl I'm going to marry.

BRENT: *(sourly)* What you'll get out of it isn't worth what you'll get into!

D.A.: *(to Brent)* My advice to you is to keep that Manton girl out of your affairs.

BRENT: *(bitterly)* She's probably the type of dame that'd come back and haunt me, otherwise I'd shoot to kill!

They start out of the office. The secretary, forgetting the large pin, sits down. He leaps to his feet with a shriek. Brent ducks as though

53

struck, whirls, then sees what it is. With a look of disgust he exits with Peter.

INTERIOR MELSA'S BEDROOM—NIGHT
Melsa is in front of vanity preparing for bed, creaming face. Kit is lying, fully clothed on the bed—she seems very tired. Lee is at the telephone.

LEE: *(to Melsa)* It's Pat—she says her feet are worn down to the ankles—

MELSA: Tell her to go home and start looking again in the morning.

LEE: *(into phone)* Pack in for the night and start again in the morning.
Myra enters.

MYRA: I wasn't in when your message came—I was...

KIT: *(finishing for her)* Out with pipsqueak.

LEE: Did you give in to that worm?

MYRA: He caught me in a weak moment and...I feel sorry for him.

HELEN: *(entering and having heard last line)* Does he love you for your looks, your brains, or your money?

KIT: One thing at a time, Helen, one thing at a time.

HELEN: *(pushing Kit)* Move over—there's been no feeling in my legs below the knees for an hour.

MYRA: *(to Melsa)* Well, what did you want?

LEE: Now that she's torn herself away, tell her, Melsa.

MELSA: We're looking for Sheila Lane—I don't believe she's been murdered, I think she's hiding from the police—afraid because she knows too much. Now of what was Sheila Lane proudest?

MYRA: Her marriage license.

KIT: *(with a laugh)* She should have been but she wasn't.

HELEN: *(patiently to Myra)* Her red hair, darling—she was proudest of her flaming topper.

MELSA: She used the same beauty shop I do—I found out her hair dresser rinsed her hair in an imported preparation very few shops use. If that peacock is alive, she's getting the stuff somewhere—this time it's find the hair preparation and you'll find the woman.

MYRA: I'm getting tired—why don't we just call in the police?

LEE: Shades preserve us, the girl is growing a brain.

MYRA: I'm getting so scared, I'm beginning to see faces over my

54

shoulder.

HELEN: It's only that college boy of yours leering at you.

MELSA: *(quietly)* If any of you girls feel like pulling out—go ahead.

LEE: Don't feel that way about it, Melsa.

HELEN: I hate the color yellow.

MELSA: There's no disgrace in being frightened.

MYRA: We'll stick.

> *Lee and Kit nod. Hilda enters.*

HILDA: All you chilluns run along now an' get some sleep. *(to Melsa)* You gowan an' get your shower.

MELSA: *(to Myra)* Myra—you take all the beauty shops along Eighth and Ninth Avenues from Fourteenth Street to Ninety-Eighth Street— the rest of you girls know your routes.

> *She places a towel around her head and exits to shower. Girls start out.*

KIT: Melsa certainly wants her pound of flesh.

LEE: Are you sure she doesn't want the one hundred and fifty-five pounds of it?

HELEN: Quiet, you carrions!

> *The girls exit. Hilda stares after them, then starts cleaning up. She mutters to herself as she works.*

HILDA: *(muttering)* Girls, girls, all they think about nowadays is men! *(thinks for a moment, then:)* And then again, why not? They make awful good thinking!

> *We hear the shower go on. The telephone rings. Hilda shuffles over to the phone and picks up the receiver.*
> *Close shot—Hilda.*

HILDA: *(continued) (into phone)* Who dere dis time of night?

INTERIOR TELEPHONE BOOTH—NIGHT
A middle-aged, determined-looking man is at the phone. He has a hard, merciless quality in his voice.

MAN: I wanna talk to Melsa Manton.

INTERIOR MELSA'S BEDROOM—NIGHT
Close shot—Hilda at phone.

HILDA: She cain't talk to you now. *(a pause)* Why not? 'Cos she's all wet—she's in the shower.

INTERIOR PHONE BOOTH—NIGHT
Close shot—man at phone.

MAN: *(curtly)* I gotta message for her. Tell her she'd better not try to find Sheila Lane or she'll wake up one morning on the bottom of the East River.

HILDA'S VOICE: *(in a scared tone)* Yes, suh—

MAN: And if she says one word to the police when they pick her up she'll assay two pounds of lead to the square inch! Get it!

INTERIOR MELSA'S BEDROOM—NIGHT
Close shot—Hilda at phone, shaking.

HILDA: Yes, suh, yes, suh, I hears you. No, suh, I ain't arguin' with you. Good-bye, suh, please.

She hangs up, gazes around the room in fear, starts for the bathroom, stops, turns, and goes back to the phone.

HILDA: *(continued) (into phone)* Hello, give me the *Morning Clarion.* I don't know no number except policy numbers. You give me the *Morning Clarion!*

INTERIOR PETER'S OFFICE—NIGHT
Peter is sitting gloomily in a chair, while the owner of the newspaper is walking up and down the room rapidly.

OWNER: *(angrily)* A fine editor I have! First you get us in a suit with her, then you let her make a monkey out of you.

PETER: *(quietly)* Do you want my resignation?

OWNER: Now, Ames, stop playing the sensitive soul. You're editor of this paper, not a crummy reporter—You're supposed to be...

PETER: —dignified, unbiased, open minded and *underpaid*—

OWNER: You're being paid to edit. Your place is behind that desk.

PETER: You're going to get your money's worth—my place is behind this desk and behind this desk I stay.

The phone rings. Peter picks it up.

PETER: *(continued) (into phone)* Yes, yes, Hilda. *(he sits up)* What? What! WHAT!!! I'll be right over.

Peter, white-faced, jumps up, runs to a rack and grabs his hat and coat, then rushes to a drawer and takes out a pistol.

PETER: *(continued) (into phone)* Get Lieutenant Brent at headquarters. Have him get down to Melsa Manton's apartment. Tell him I'll explain why later. *(he dashes out)*

OWNER: *(protesting)* But you said you...

DISSOLVE

INTERIOR MELSA'S BEDROOM—NIGHT

Peter bursts into the room. Hilda, in dressing gown, waddles in behind him. Peter flashes the light on and rushes to the bed. Melsa is lying sprawled on the bed, one hand hanging over the bed, her hair streaming over the side of the bed. She is wearing a night shade. Peter gets down on his knees, gathers her in his arms and starts to blubber.

PETER: Melsa—Melsa! My darling! What have they done to you?

Melsa wakes up suddenly, startled. She pushes Peter away and cries out.

MELSA: *(frightened)* Hilda! Hilda!

She snatches the night shade from her eyes and recognizes Peter.

MELSA: *(continued)* Oh, it's you!

PETER: *(relieved)* Darling, you're not dead!

MELSA: *(puzzled and annoyed)* Are you disappointed?

PETER: You gave me the fright of my life. Do you always sleep this way?

MELSA: Yes.

Hilda stands in the doorway, watching them.

PETER: Something will have to be done about it. I can't stand a fright like this every day.

MELSA: *(very coldly)* I assume you had a reason for bursting in this way—or is it spring?

PETER: That threat—that threat over the phone... *(standing up)* I'm spending the night right here.

MELSA: *(looking him over icily)* In my lifetime I've heard of a variety of subterfuges—Japanese robes, rare ivory, a view of the Hudson—but, Ames, you're superb! No other man in the whole world could have thought of this. *(in a disbelieving tone)* What threat?

PETER: The threat Hilda got.

Melsa turns to Hilda questioningly.

MELSA: *(to Hilda)* Do you mean to tell me you couldn't recognize this charlatan's voice? Hilda, for the last time, you're fired!

HILDA: Twasn't this lad's voice—He done said if you tole the police he'd erase you.

PETER: Rub her out, Hilda, *rub* her out.

HILDA: Yes, sir—dat's what he done said.

MELSA: You see, he even remembers his exact words.

PETER: *(to Melsa, seriously)* You're up to your beautiful hips in murder. This isn't a society tea. You're fooling with someone who isn't afraid to kill. Who is he? What are you girls up to? Men don't go around threatening to kill without a reason. Please tell me.

MELSA: *(tauntingly)* Wouldn't you and Brent like to know!

PETER: Remember I once said I'd beat that nastiness out of you—do you want me to start now?

HILDA: Ah'd better go.

MELSA: *(frantically)* Hilda, you stay here.

PETER: *(determinedly)* I'm staying right here until Brent shows up.

HILDA: But dat—dat man done said not to bring the police.

MELSA: *(to Peter)* You can go out and stay in the living room.

PETER: *(shaking his head)* I'm not letting you out of my sight.

MELSA: Hilda can sleep in here.

Peter turns and walks over to Hilda.

PETER: All right, Hilda. *(holding out his gun)* Can you handle a gun?

HILDA: *(drawing back frightened)* No, Ah cain't—I's a paci*fus!*

PETER: *(turning to Melsa)* You see? You'd better go back to sleep. I'll lie down here on the couch.

He sits down on the couch. Hilda goes, being careful to leave the door open.

PETER: *(continued)* Do you want the light on or off?

MELSA: It doesn't make any difference to me. I sleep with a night shade. *(she puts it on, lies down in bed)* Good night.

PETER: Good night.

There is a silence in the room. Peter gazes at the window, at the pictures on the walls, at the ashtrays; in fact, he gazes at everything in the room except the bed. He gets up, puts light out. Street light pours into room.

Medium close shot. Peter is having a difficult time. He is fidgety. He bends his knees a little, decides that isn't comfortable, then turns over on his other side. Finally, he settles on his back and gazes up at the ceiling. After a few minutes he takes out a cigarette and lights it with a lighter. He takes a few puffs. Suddenly we hear Melsa's voice.

MELSA'S VOICE: May I have a cigarette, please?

Medium shot. Peter gets up, walks over to Melsa's bed. She has sleep shade off. He hands her a cigarette. There is now a different atmosphere in the room. Both are intently aware of their own emotions. He lights the lighter and bends over Melsa to light her cigarette. The light flickers, revealing Melsa's face. Her expression is somewhat tremulous.

MELSA: *(continued) (hesitantly, trying to cover up her feelings)* I've had dozens of cigarette lighters, but they never work.

PETER: *(also obviously disguising his true emotions)* Well, this one does, I use cheap gasoline.

MELSA: Maybe that's why it works.

Peter lights Melsa's cigarette. Her hand trembles a little, and Peter takes it in his to steady it. He holds it for a while, then lets go and walks to the window. He leans against the side of the window looking out. There is a little silence between them.

PETER: *(still intent on small talk; anything to stay away from the subject nearest his heart)* Funny thing about street lights at night—you never notice them, but they're so bright, and constant, too—They were out last night—tonight—and tomorrow they'll be there again.

MELSA: *(also making small talk)* Yes, I suppose this city is in a rut.

(None of this scene is flip. It is just two people talking around a subject they dare not mention to each other.)

PETER: I once smashed a street light—it was for a lady, she asked me to do it—I was five then and very much in love.

MELSA: *(gazing intently at Peter)* Was she pretty?

PETER: The cutest thing you ever saw. Our parents thought we were too young to be thinking of that sort of thing, so they shipped her off to kindergarten.

59

MELSA: Whatever became of her?

PETER: She's probably still in kindergarten.

There is a silence again. Melsa looks at Peter, then she gets up, puts a wrap over her, and walks to the window. She stands at the opposite side of the window and looks out at the street.

PETER: *(continued) (acutely aware of her presence, yet staring out of window)* I couldn't live in this apartment—it's too high up for me—I've got acrophobia.

MELSA: What's that?

PETER: A fear of high places.

MELSA: Do you get sort of sick inside?

PETER: Like I've suddenly become empty.

MELSA: Me, too—that's why I never go out on the balcony.

PETER: I couldn't stand it.

They are moving closer to each other.

MELSA: Neither could I. That's why I don't go out there.

PETER: I get the same feeling when I ride in an elevator.

MELSA: Up or down?

PETER: Up.

MELSA: I feel like that both ways.

They are quite close now.

PETER: We have a lot in common, haven't we?

MELSA: *(a little frightened at what is about to occur)* All except the elevator.

PETER: Melsa... Melsa...

MELSA: Yes...

PETER: Melsa...

MELSA: What?

PETER: I'm terribly worried about you. Will you please tell me who this man is who's threatening you? Who is he?

Melsa looks at him. Her eyes harden. She flips the light on, walks to the door and opens it.

MELSA: *(turning to Peter, very quietly)* Good night, Mr. Ames.

PETER: *(protesting)* I swear I'm only concerned about you.

MELSA: Good night.

PETER: I'm not going—not until—

The telephone bell rings. Melsa answers it.

MELSA: Hello—yes...yes, Dora.

INTERIOR TELEPHONE BOOTH—NIGHT
On Dora. She is very excited.

DORA: Ah dun found her, Melsa, Ah dun found her! The beauty-parlah girl paid me no mind at first—but Ah dun give her a peek at a hundred dollahs—Jumpin' catfish—does ma feet ache—Ah walked an' walked...

INTERIOR MELSA'S APARTMENT—NIGHT
On Melsa.

MELSA: Will you take that Mason-Dixon line out of your mouth and talk English!

INTERIOR TELEPHONE BOOTH—NIGHT
On Dora.

DORA: Well, Ah paid that beauty operatah a hundred dollars and she described Sheila an' tole me where at she's livin'—it's the Ashton Hotel right on Twenty-third Street. She calls herself Sharon Lester.

INTERIOR MELSA'S APARTMENT—NIGHT
On Melsa.

MELSA: *(into phone)* Thanks, Dora. *(she hangs up; to Peter)* You can stay here. I'm spending the night with Dora—she...er...she just invited me—that was Dora on the phone.

She walks to the closet, reaches for a fur coat, and throws it over her, Peter pleading with her all the while.

PETER: *(pleading)* You can't do it. You can't go out in the street by yourself. Not until Brent arrives.

Melsa takes a hat from a table, puts it on, and exits. Peter follows her, as we

WIPE

EXTERIOR MELSA'S APARTMENT BUILDING—NIGHT
Melsa enters scene from apartment house. Peter, still protesting, follows her.

PETER: At least let me take you there.

A car drives up—Brent and two men are in it.

BRENT: *(inside of car, calls out)* Pete!

PETER: *(looking towards him)* Oh, Mike, I'm glad you're here.

> *Melsa starts down the street as Peter starts for the car. Suddenly another car, containing two men, comes tearing around the corner. The car screeches past and a gun pops. Peter falls to the sidewalk. The revolving door is shattered. Urns at the side of the entrance fall to the street. Melsa stops and screams. Brent and the detectives jump out of their car and fire at the speeding automobile. The fleeing car sluices up the sidewalk and crashes into a glass store window. Brent and the detectives start running over to the crashed car. Melsa runs over to Peter.*

MELSA: *(bending over Peter)* Peter!

EXTERIOR STREET—NIGHT

Medium shot. The car stands among the wreckage of the window. Two men climb out of overturned car—one quickly throws something away. We recognize the man who threatened Melsa. Brent and men run into scene, grab other two. The other captive is the driver of Regan's car.

REGAN: *(snarling)* Let go, copper, or I'll—

BRENT: *(looking at him)* Bat Regan!

REGAN: Who'd you think it was—Kris Kringle?

BRENT: Why did you do it?

REGAN: *(still snarling)* I'm class-conscious, see! I don't like society dames!

> *Policeman runs in.*

POLICEMAN: I sent for the ambulance, Chief—he's bleeding bad.

> *Sullivan picks up a wallet.*

SULLIVAN: Here's what he threw away, Chief.

BRENT: *(taking wallet)* Throwing away dough!

REGAN: The recession is over—things are humming again.

> *Brent looks through money.*

BRENT: Twenty grand—you didn't happen to get this from Lane? *(chidingly)* Now before you fib—we've got the numbers from the bank.

REGAN: He lost it to me over one of my roulette tables.

> *Brent slaps Regan across the face.*

BRENT: There's nothing lower than a dirty murdering blackmailer.

REGAN: With my arms being held you're pretty tough.

Brent nods to the policemen who let Regan's arms go. He puts them up. Brent slugs him on the chin. Regan goes down.

BRENT: Trying to escape, eh!

There's the sound of the clanging ambulance.

POLICEMAN: There's the ambulance for Ames.

They turn.

DISSOLVE

INTERIOR HOSPITAL CORRIDOR—NIGHT

Our group of girls are seated outside a sickroom door. They are quiet, gloomy, tense. Melsa is lacing up and down the corridor nervously. Helen gets up and walks over to Melsa.

HELEN: Melsa, please. Melsa, please cry. Why don't you cry? That'll help.

Melsa shakes her head, pushes Helen away, and starts pacing again.

INTERIOR HOSPITAL ROOM—NIGHT

Peter—a healthy-looking Peter—is sitting up in bed. An intern is sticking plaster on his shoulder. Peter has a tray in front of him and is eating a hearty meal—steak, potatoes, vegetables, and pie are on the tray. Brent is standing by the bed watching.

INTERN: *(to Peter)* There you are. In a day or two, you'll be as good as new.

PETER: *(to intern)* Thanks a lot.

The intern walks to the door and exits.

BRENT: *(to Peter, exasperated)* All we could get out of Regan was the money came to him from Lane in a game. I think it was blackmail and when Lane threatened to go to the police, he killed him. Belden saw it, so he killed Belden.

PETER: Why should he shoot at Melsa?

BRENT: He says he was cleaning the gun and it went off!

PETER: *(amused)* Cleaning a gun in a car?

BRENT: It's Regan's gun and he insists it's his privilege to clean it wherever he likes. I'm trying to hold on to him but they've set his bail at a hundred thousand—Regan will have it up in twenty-four hours.

PETER: Fine thing.

BRENT: Now, Regan was the guy who threatened Manton and shot at her, and I want to know why. That girl knows something we don't know—otherwise, Regan wouldn't have tried to kill her. If he won't tell us, we'll have to get it out of Manton.

PETER: *(with a dry laugh)* Get something out of Manton? Don't make me laugh! This steak is too good to choke on. *(taking another bite of steak)*

BRENT: Listen, Pete, I told her you were dying and she's out there in the corridor crying her head off for you.

PETER: She is? That's worth dying for—well, almost worth dying for.

BRENT: Listen, in the condition she's in, she'd even tell you her age, if you asked it. You can get anything out of her if she thinks you're dying.

> *The door starts opening and we see the back of a cop stopping Melsa who is trying to force her way into the room.*

COP (SULLIVAN): I'm sorry, you can't get in, lady.

MELSA: *(struggling with him; wide-eyed)* I must see him! I must see him!

> *Brent grabs the tray and shoves it under the bed. Peter slumps under the covers and pulls the sheets over him.*

BRENT: *(to Sullivan)* Let her in, Sullivan.

> *Brent assumes a woebegone look. Sullivan steps aside and lets Melsa in, then he steps into the room and stands beside the door. Melsa runs over to Peter.*

BRENT: *(continued)* Don't tax him too much. He's sinking fast.

MELSA: *(bending over Peter)* Darling, oh, darling!

PETER: *(his eyes closed, his voice a whisper)* Who is it?

MELSA: It's Melsa, darling. What have they done to you, darling?

PETER: They've killed me.

BRENT: *(emoting)* The rats!

MELSA: No, they haven't, dear. You'll live—you've got to live— *(bravely)* You've got to get strong and well for your career—for your future.

PETER: Future—*(with a sigh that is the quintessence of futility, followed by a forced chuckle of self-pity to think that fate has dealt him such an ugly blow; more softly)* Future—

MELSA: Yes—our future. You've promised before witnesses that you'd marry me—you've got to live—I love you.

She drops her head to the bed.

PETER: *(overjoyed)* She loves me. *(he rears up in joy)*

Brent pushes him down, accidentally touching his wound.

PETER: *(continued)* O-o-o-o-h!

Melsa raises her head in surprise.

BRENT: Just the first death rattle.

PETER: *(to Melsa, weakly, with a wan smile)* Who is it that said joy always comes to a man too late?

Sullivan at door starts sniffling.

MELSA: *(shaking her head frantically)* Oh, no, no. No!

BRENT: *(an innuendo in his tone)* Pete—Pete, boy, don't you want us to avenge you? *(he signals to Peter over Melsa's head)*

Peter in his enjoyment of the scene has forgotten all about the idea of extracting information from Melsa.

PETER: No, Mike, I forgive everybody.

SULLIVAN: *(sniffling)* That's what I call a nice guy!

BRENT: *(trying to get the idea over to Peter)* Even the rat who shot you?

PETER: Even him, Mike.

BRENT: *(trying to get a lot of meaning into his words)* Wouldn't— wouldn't you rest easier—if you knew why he did it—just out of curiosity?

MELSA: *(brokenly)* What good would it do us? It's all my fault, and now I'm going to be all alone.

PETER: Mike, you know that Melsa wouldn't hold anything back from a dying man.

SULLIVAN: *(tearfully)* Mr. Ames, isn't there something I can do for you?

PETER: Yes, Sullivan. Will you sing my favorite song for me? "Home on the Range."

SULLIVAN: Sure.

He starts to sing "Home, Home on the Range." Brent takes off his hat. Sullivan, as he sings, does the same.

PETER: *(wistfully)* Never to see the sun again. *(suddenly his voice rises in revolt)* I don't want to die! I'm too young to die! I want to feel the rain in my face, the wind in my hair. I want to smell the good earth.

MELSA: Oh, Peter, Peter!

PETER: *(softly, to Melsa)* We could have made sweet music together.

BRENT: *(beginning to recite, softly)* "He rose like a meteor—flashed

65

across our sky, and then was gone."

PETER: *(smiling wanly at Brent in appreciation)* Good-bye, Mike.

BRENT: *(working up to a sob)* I'm not going to take this lying down. You are my friend, my best friend and—*(pointedly)*—and if it's no interest to Miss Manton, it is to me. I must have my revenge! *(turning to Melsa)* Why, why, did Regan shoot at you, Miss Manton, WHY?

MELSA: We were looking for Sheila Lane—he threatened to kill me if I didn't stop.

PETER: And—did—you—find—her—dear?

MELSA: Yes, she's registered as Sharon Lester at the Ashton Hotel on Twenty-third Street.

Brent tries to conceal a look of gratification.

BRENT: *(to Peter, forgetting himself)* Well, I'll be seeing you—*(quickly)* I mean when my number is called.

He strides to the door. Sullivan is still singing softly, "Home on the Range."

BRENT: *(continued) (to Sullivan, out of the side of his mouth)* That's enough, Sullivan—quite enough. *(he motions to Sullivan to follow him out)*

INTERIOR HOSPITAL CORRIDOR—NIGHT

Medium shot as Brent and Sullivan come out.

BRENT: *(to a nurse)* Where's a phone?

NURSE: Down the corridor on the floor desk.

Brent hurriedly starts down the corridor.

INTERIOR HOSPITAL ROOM—NIGHT

Melsa, who is weeping wildly, puts her head on the side of the bed. Camera pans down to the floor following Melsa's gaze. She sees on the floor the tray of food—a half-eaten steak, the French fried potatoes, the vegetables, and the pie.

Camera pans up and moves in to a close two-shot. We see Melsa's face harden as she realizes she has been duped, and then it softens into a new kind of concern.

MELSA: *(her face is all tenderness)* Are you still in pain—? *(her face changes to hate and her voice is vehement; she reaches under the bed and gets a firm grip on the fork)*—sweet?

66

At the sharpness of the word "sweet," Peter quickly opens his eyes, but Melsa's face is again reverted to that expression of angelic sweetness.

PETER: It's—it's nothing, darling—only when I move. *(he shifts his body an inch and winces gallantly)* But it's nothing.

MELSA: Oh, Peter, perhaps I did wrong in not telling Inspector Brent everything.

PETER: You mean you've held something back?

MELSA: Yes, Peter.

PETER: Oh, sweet—you're so clever.

MELSA: Remember when I went into Ronnie Belden's apartment?

PETER: Yes, dear.

MELSA: When I went into the bathroom—I found something.

PETER: In the bathroom?

MELSA: —Floating around—in a foot of water in the bath tub.

PETER: Louder, sweet—you sound so far away,

MELSA: *(grasps fork from Peter's dinner tray under the bed)* I'll come closer—And when I saw it—floating so helplessly in a tub so small, I couldn't understand how it even got there.

PETER: *(very anxious)* Tell me, dear—what was it?

MELSA: *(building her speech to a crescendo)* THE NORMANDIE, YOU BLACK-HEARTED FAKER—IN FULL SAIL!!!

Melsa jabs the fork under the covers into Peter. He jumps with pain.

PETER: Ouch!

Melsa strides out of room.

FADE OUT

FADE IN

INTERIOR BRENT'S OFFICE—DAY

It is day, but the blinds are drawn—a bright light in the center of the room shines directly down at a woman who sits under it. We recognize Sheila Lane. Detectives, police and Brent lean against the wall, in the shadows. All eyes are on Sheila. There is a long silence in the room. Sheila is distraught.

67

SHEILA: *(finally bursting out at them)* Why do you stare at me that way—why do you . . . *(her voice catches, she covers her mouth with a handkerchief)*

BRENT: Why did you hide from the police, Mrs. Lane?

SHEILA: I didn't hide from the police. I was afraid whoever killed George and Ronnie would kill me. I went to Bat Regan—I used to work for him; he loved me and would do anything for me. He owns that hotel I was at. He hid me—gave me money to live on.

BRENT: Your husband's money—blackmail money. Why did you help Regan blackmail your husband?

SHEILA: Blackmail! But blackmailing—I don't believe it!

BRENT: You were married to a convict before you married your husband, weren't you?

SHEILA: Haven't *you* ever made a mistake—when you were young?

BRENT: *(disregarding her question)* Through Regan you blackmailed your own husband. When he found out about it, you killed him.

SHEILA: *(begging)* Please, please—I told you I came to the old house *after* my husband was dead—Ronnie and I had been meeting there—that's why you found my clip. Ronnie told me he'd seen my husband murdered. He didn't want to go to the police—it would have exposed our relationship. He told me to leave and he'd take the body—drop it somewhere else—he didn't want it discovered where . . . where we had been meeting. He must have taken the body out while the Manton girl was calling the police—then before he could get rid of it, he was killed.

BRENT: Don't you mean that Belden loved you enough to get rid of the body for you?

SHEILA: No!

BRENT: Maybe he helped you murder your husband because he'd found out about both of you—then you murdered Belden because he knew too much.

SHEILA: *(softly crying)* Lieutenant Brent—there isn't very much left of my life—I really don't care what you do to me—do as you please.

BRENT: Very touching Mrs. Lane—but unfortunately it's the same line Magda Dufree, the hammer murderer, used the moment before we pulled the switch. Take her back to her cell.

    She is led out.

INTERIOR BOOKING ROOM AT HEADQUARTERS—NIGHT
A large group of seedy, unkempt-looking vagrants are standing before the desk sergeant, surrounded by cops. The desk sergeant from his eminence above them is belaboring the vagrants.

DESK SERGEANT: I'm not going to book you guys, because you ain't criminals. But that doesn't mean we're going to let you hang around. This city is providing work for . . .

The outside door opens and Melsa steps into the room, dressed in an extreme-style evening dress. She starts walking across the room toward Brent's office. The sergeant stops talking and every man in the room—vagrants, cops, and the desk sergeant—follows her with his eyes as she trips across the room, opens the door to Brent's office, and exits. Then, as with one motion, their heads turn back to their former positions.

DESK SERGEANT: *(continued)* *(staring at the door, then recalling himself)* Now, where was I? Oh, yeah—*(he bends down and points an accusing finger at the vagrants)* This city is providing work . . .

INTERIOR BRENT'S OFFICE—NIGHT
Brent is lighting Melsa's cigarette. Detectives are standing around the room. Melsa is seated in an armchair.

BRENT: *(to Melsa; very courteous)* Is this chair comfortable?

MELSA: It's very comfortable, thank you.

BRENT: *(holding out pillow)* How about a pillow?

MELSA: No, thank you.

SULLIVAN: *(holding out a cigar)* Have a cigar? *(then remembers it's a female)*

BRENT: *(smiling at her)* Now, Miss Manton, as you know, you've been a great help to us.

Melsa opens her mouth to say something.

BRENT: *(continued)* Oh, yes, you have! We may have had our little disagreements, but then, who doesn't?

Peter walks in. When Melsa sees him, she gets up, and turns to Brent.

MELSA: *(coldly)* Good evening, Inspector.

She takes a step to the door.

BRENT: *(hurriedly)* Now, Miss Manton, because you don't like Ames

69

here, don't allow it to undermine the good work you've been doing.

PETER: I didn't know you were going to be here. Brent sent for me.

Melsa looks at Peter for a moment, then returns to her chair, and sits down. He takes a chair and sits down, but leaps up—the spot in which Melsa stabbed him is still sore. A satisfied look crosses Melsa's face.

MELSA: All right, Inspector. Why did you send for me?

Brent draws up a chair beside Melsa and sits with his knees almost touching hers. He leans forward confidentially.

BRENT: Here's the idea, Miss Manton. You saw Ronnie Belden come out of the Lane house, didn't you?

MELSA: Yes.

BRENT: Everybody knows you're mixed up in this—collected evidence—everybody suspects you of holding out—even *I* do.

MELSA: I'll bet you say that to all the girls.

BRENT: *(with intense seriousness)* Now, what would happen if we published the fact that you had just uncovered some new evidence which is certain to lead to the discovery of the murderer, and that you have an appointment with the district attorney tomorrow to turn over the evidence to him.

MELSA: *(with a slight shudder)* I'd probably be found in a refrigerator.

BRENT: Correct, that's just what we want.

MELSA: *(rising and starting for door)* Isn't it lucky I didn't find any new evidence?

BRENT: *(pleading)* We'll give you all the protection you need. All you have to do is to appear in public with Pete where the murderer can get at you. First, I'll surround you with police, then release the suspects.

MELSA: *(turning on Peter and very quietly)* Are you willing to have me do this?

PETER: *(seriously)* There's a homicidal maniac loose somewhere—and, anyway, sooner or later he's going to think you know too much. I'd rather be there when he makes the attempt.

MELSA: Well, Mr. Ames, you *are* unique in the manner in which you date a girl.

PETER: *(with a shrug)* If any other of your men friends is willing to escort you under those circumstances...

BRENT: Take a little time to think it over.

MELSA: Thank you very much. I'm going to Europe pretty soon. I'll be back in the fall and we can talk it over.

PETER: *(to Brent)* Mike, she's right.

BRENT: *(turning to Peter)* Look, Pete, I'm a cop, and funny enough I like being a cop, but there have been lots of things I've had to do that made me hate policemen, including myself—*(putting his hand on Peter's arm and speaking very earnestly)*—and this is one of the times. But there's a killer loose—

PETER: Let me ask you something, Mike. If it was your wife, would you do this?

MELSA: Inspector, that's an implication that I'm his wife, and I'm not.

BRENT: *(softly)* Yes, Pete, if she was my wife I would, because I think that millions of other wives have the right to live in safety from murderers. *(turning to Melsa)* Will you do it?

PETER: No, she won't! I won't let her!

Melsa is annoyed at Peter for speaking for her.

MELSA: *(to Peter)* You won't let me! You're scared because he's asking you to be there, too. *(to Brent)* This proves there's insanity in my family—I'll do it!

BRENT: *(quietly)* Thanks.

MELSA: But that doesn't mean we're friends. If I get a chance to take your badge away from you, I'm going to do it!

BRENT: *(sincerely)* Just catch that killer, and you can have my badge. *(to detectives)* Release Sheila Lane—the rest of them are loose—Regan got his bail this morning. *(to Peter)* Now, get on the phone to your paper and release a story about Melsa finding the new evidence.

Peter makes a gesture of resignation, picks up the phone, and starts to dial.

PETER: *(to Melsa)* Scared? Because I am!

MELSA: *(her teeth chattering, her hands shaking)* I'm not scared. *(pulling at her handkerchief nervously)* If I'm dead tomorrow morning, will you call the Hayden Beauty Parlor? I've an appointment with my hairdresser, and they're very strict about keeping appointments. *(suddenly she begins to cry)*

The men look on sympathetically.

PETER: *(into phone)* Hello ... Ames—get me re-write.

71

DISSOLVE OUT

DISSOLVE IN

INTERIOR ONE-ARM LUNCH COUNTER—NIGHT
Medium shot—Norris, seated on one of the stools, is reading the newspaper headline:

> MELSA MANTON TO REVEAL NEW EVIDENCE
> TO DISTRICT ATTORNEY
> ARREST EXPECTED IN 24 HOURS

WIPE

INTERIOR BEAUTY PARLOR—NIGHT
Sheila Lane, her hair under the dryer, her face covered with creams, is reading the same newspaper headline.

WIPE

EXTERIOR CORNER NEWSSTAND—NIGHT
Thomas, a newspaper in his hand, is just tossing a few coins to the newspaper vendor. He starts to read the same newspaper headline.

WIPE

INTERIOR SUBWAY CAR—NIGHT
Frances Glesk, holding onto a strap, is reading the same headline over a man's shoulder.

WIPE

INTERIOR POOLROOM—NIGHT
Bat Regan, a cue stick in one hand, has a newspaper in the other hand.
(NOTE: All the people in these scenes have enigmatic looks on their faces.)

INTERIOR APARTMENT—NIGHT
Girls reading the paper over each others' shoulders.

DISSOLVE OUT

DISSOLVE IN

EXTERIOR CHEZ LUIS NIGHTCLUB—NIGHT
People in evening dress are entering the nightclub. A uniformed doorman is at the door. Down the street a short distance a cab stands. A taxicab draws up at the curb and Peter and Melsa, in evening dress, step out. Peter pays the driver. They start to cross over to the entrance.
Close shot—another car driving down the street. It backfires.
Full shot—on the sidewalk outside the entrance to the nightclub. Peter steps in front of Melsa and tries to shield her. The doorman makes a grab for her and pulls out a gun. From the cab four detectives come running out. From all sides and directions men come running over and surround Melsa.
Medium shot—Peter looks around.
PETER: It's all right, boys. It was just a car backfiring.
DOORMAN: *(releasing Melsa)* Rafferty, from headquarters, Miss. You don't have to worry. We're all around you.
PETER: All right. Come along, Melsa.
He starts for the door. Melsa runs after him, takes his arm and hugs it tightly—scared. They exit into the nightclub.

INTERIOR NIGHTCLUB—NIGHT
Medium shot—at hatcheck counter. The hatcheck girl stands behind the counter. Peter and Melsa enter scene. Melsa still has Peter by the arm. He hands his hat to the girl.
PETER: *(turning to Melsa)* I'd like to get my arm out of that sleeve, if you don't mind.
MELSA: Oh, excuse me.
She lets go his arm. Peter hands his coat to the hatcheck girl, then offers his arm to Melsa.
MELSA: *(continued)* It's quite all right.

PETER: *(unconcerned)* Okay.
He starts down the hall. Once more Melsa runs after him and grabs his arm, holding onto it tightly.

INTERIOR NIGHTCLUB DANCE FLOOR—NIGHT
The usual nightclub scene. Tables are crowded around the dance floor; people in evening dress; orchestra playing a dance number. Peter and Melsa come into scene escorted by the headwaiter, who seats them. He hands them a menu, then snaps his fingers for a waiter, and leaves. In a moment the waiter comes over.
PETER: *(to waiter)* How's the terrapin tonight?
WAITER: I dunno. I'll ask the guy in the kitchen.
Peter and Melsa exchange looks.
PETER: *(to waiter)* Never mind, we'll take the dinner.
WAITER: Oke—coming up. *(he writes something on a pad)*
PETER: *(glancing at the wine list)* Have you Chablis, '29?
WAITER: What's Chablis, '29?
Peter and Melsa once again exchange puzzled glances. A drunk staggers by and bumps against Melsa's chair. Peter immediately jumps up. The waiter reaches into his vest and has his gun halfway out.
DRUNK: 'Scuse me.
He stumbles off. Peter looks at the waiter.
WAITER: Driscoll—headquarters. Everything's under control. I'll get your chow. *(he starts out)*
PETER: *(to waiter, in a low voice)* Just a minute. Before you get our dinners, is the chef a headquarters man, too?
WAITER: *(in a low voice)* Naw.
PETER: Okay.
The waiter leaves. The orchestra is playing a dance number. Peter leans across the table.
PETER: *(continued) (to Melsa)* Dance?
MELSA: *(her voice still scared)* No.
PETER: All right.
He gets up and starts walking to the dance floor. Melsa immediately jumps up and runs to him, grabbing his arm. They start to dance.

74

Moving shot as Peter and Melsa dance. Peter is holding Melsa very tightly.

MELSA: *(coldly)* Is it necessary for you to hold me so tightly?

She pushes him away from her.

PETER: Of course, you make a better target by yourself.

Melsa immediately steps up close to him again. They dance a few steps.

MELSA: Why don't you draw red circles around me and rent me out to a rifle range?

They dance a few steps.

PETER: *(softly)* That wasn't the real reason I was holding you so close. It so happens—heaven help me!—I love you.

MELSA: You're taking unfair advantage of me. The only reason I'm here with you is because—there's a gun in my back.

PETER: Lots of times those marriages turn out very well.

Peter and Melsa dance past the orchestra stand. Suddenly there is a sour note from the cornet player.

Medium shot—at orchestra stand. The leader glares at the cornet player. The cornet player winks off at Peter and Melsa.

Close shot—Peter and Melsa on the floor see the cornet player wink, and look at each other.

Close shot of cornet player. Camera pans down revealing a hand machine gun resting between the cornet player's knees. He holds the machine gun with one hand and plays the cornet with the other.

Medium shot—on dance floor.

MELSA: *(whispering fiercely)* I'm going to become hysterical in a moment!—I've got the jitters!—I know I'm going to burst into crazy laughter!—Say something to stop me. Make me feel sad!

PETER: *(trying to stop her)* There's nothing to laugh at—and besides I wish you could have a look at yourself. You look awful! Your complexion's terrible! You look like a witch! Is that sad enough for you?

MELSA: *(furiously)* You don't have to sound as if you mean it. You don't look so good yourself.

The orchestra finishes playing, and couples start walking back to their tables. The lights go out, leaving only a spotlight on the dance floor. A girl in dancing costume comes out and goes into a dance number.

75

Close shot—Peter and Melsa sit down at their table. Suddenly a shot is heard, and the wine bottle on the table is smashed to bits. Women scream. Melsa slides under the table. Peter drops down beneath the table.

Full shot—Another shot is heard, and the spotlight on the dance floor goes out. There are screams, shouts, cries, noise of tables being overturned. We hear detectives' voices ad libbing.

AD LIBS: Get the door, Mac.

Where are the lights?

Don't move, anybody! *etc., etc.*

The lights go on revealing the room in great disorder. Brent dashes into the room with uniformed police. The detectives in the room are herding people together.

BRENT: Get them all down to headquarters.

Peter is looking under the table.

Medium shot—under table. Peter is on his hands and knees looking around. Melsa is nowhere in sight.

PETER: *(alarmed)* Melsa! Melsa!

Full shot—A detective comes into the room, a machine gun under his arm. He goes over to Brent.

DETECTIVE: I don't think you'll find the murderer in here. Chief. Whoever it was got in and out through a window in the hall. I just found the latch smashed.

Peter graps Brent by the lapels.

PETER: *(hoarsely)* And he's got Melsa! It's your fault, Mike, and I'm going to break every bone in your body!

From behind a drape at a window, Melsa comes cautiously out. They all stare at her.

MELSA: Did you get him?

BRENT: *(ruefully)* I'm afraid not, Miss Manton.

PETER: I need a drink.

He snatches a bottle from a table and pours himself a stiff drink, his hand shaking. He gulps the drink down.

PETER: *(continued)* There, I feel better.

Suddenly, his knees go out from under him and he sinks into a chair.

76

DETECTIVE: *(holding out something to Brent)* I found this stuck on the window pane.

BRENT: What is it?

DETECTIVE: A hunk of tar paper. Maybe he's a roofer.

Closeup of Melsa as she looks at the tar paper in Brent's hands. She thinks for a while.

Medium group shot

MELSA: *(turning to Brent)* I'm a mess! Do you mind if I clean up in the ladies' room?

Peter gets up from the chair.

PETER: I'll go with you.

Melsa looks at him.

PETER: *(continued)* As far as the door.

Melsa and Peter start out of the room, camera trucking with them. Melsa keeps a few steps ahead of Peter.

PETER: *(continued)* *(pleading)* Melsa, I've got to take you out of all this . . .

MELSA: Wouldn't you rather wait until I've made up?

They reach a door marked "LADIES' LOUNGE." Peter stations himself outside the door.

PETER: Don't be afraid. I'm going to stay right here. Nobody's going to pass me.

Melsa starts in the door.

MELSA: *(to Peter, over her shoulder)* Isn't that being a little selfish?

She exits, leaving Peter standing there.

INTERIOR LADIES' LOUNGE—NIGHT

Melsa enters, walks over to the phone and drops in a nickel, then starts to dial. After a moment she speaks into the phone.

MELSA: *(into phone)* Hello—Helen? Melsa. Get the girls and meet me at my house. Don't ask any questions—just meet me there.

She hangs up, looks around the room, then goes to a window and opens it. As she starts to climb out the window, we

DISSOLVE

EXTERIOR STREET OUTSIDE MELSA'S APARTMENT— NIGHT

A taxi draws up to the curb. Melsa gets out and pays the cab driver. We can see from Melsa's expression that she is preoccupied. She looks down the street toward the subway excavation, then around her, etc.

Camera trucks with Melsa as she walks down the street over to the subway excavation. An unfinished kiosk marks the entrance down to the subway. All the usual paraphernalia of building is around, including a few rolls of tar paper. Melsa tears off a piece of tar paper and examines it, looks around the street once again and then finally walks into the kiosk, despite signs tacked on the kiosk which read: KEEP OUT—EXCAVATION—HIGH TENSION, *etc.*

INTERIOR SUBWAY—NIGHT

Medium shot of a half-finished platform. The train tracks are already laid. The beams are still unpainted. A few dim lights light the station. There is no tiling on the walls or floor as yet. In one corner we see a whole row of handcars. Melsa enters, looks around, then goes over and looks at the handcars. She appears lost in thought. Pan camera to shadow on wall—large shadow, gun in hand. Melsa, through corner of eyes, sees it. She gasps and whirls. Camera pulls back to include night watchman, pipe in hand. He is an old codger and carries a stick in the other hand.

WATCHMAN: This subway ain't open yet, Miss—

MELSA: Oh, I didn't...

WATCHMAN: The trains won't be running for two years yet—if we keep goin' this way.

MELSA: Oh, I... I own stock in the company. I thought I'd come down and see how things were going.

WATCHMAN: You're a stockholder—got much stock?

MELSA: Lots of it!

WATCHMAN: Well, will you speak to the board of directors and see what you kin do about gettin' me a new club—like a cop's club. This is only a stick.

MELSA: I'll get you one myself. *(points to handcar)* Do those things go very fast?

WATCHMAN: Sure do, Miss. I gotta walk—sometimes I do a little cheating—steal a ride—press a button and zip, I'm there.

MELSA: Thanks, Daddy—*(gives him a bill)* Here, buy yourself another pipe—one that looks less like a gun—Goodnight.

She turns and begins to exit.

WATCHMAN: *(calling after her)* You won't forget to talk to them directors about that club.

DISSOLVE OUT

DISSOLVE IN

INTERIOR MELSA MANTON'S APARTMENT CORRIDOR—NIGHT

As Melsa exits from the elevator toward the door of her apartment, takes key from bag, opens door. Just as she gets it open, a man who has been hiding around a turn in the corridor steps behind her and enters with her. She gives a little gasp of surprise.

MELSA: Oh, it's you, Mr. Norris. What are you doing here?

INTERIOR FOYER—NIGHT

Norris closing door behind him. He speaks quietly.

NORRIS: I've been waiting for you. You know I never did thank you properly for providing that alibi.

MELSA: *(a little nervously)* That's all right—you're welcome—and now—I'm very tired.

NORRIS: *(quietly)* I won't keep you more than a moment.

He takes her arm, begins walking her into the living room.

INTERIOR LIVING ROOM—NIGHT

As they enter.

NORRIS: Please sit down—I want to ask you about Sheila Lane. I was married to her, you know.

MELSA: *(picks up a cigarette box)* Have a cigarette?

NORRIS: Never smoke.

MELSA: Will you have a drink?

NORRIS: Never drink.

79

MELSA: Well—that's nice.

NORRIS: *(quietly)* Please sit down.

Melsa seats herself. Norris seats himself opposite.

NORRIS: *(continued)* I read in the papers that the police found Sheila Lane. You know what happened down at headquarters. Did you see her? Did you speak to her?

MELSA: *(shakes her head)* No—they let her go.

NORRIS: Are you sure?

MELSA: Well, I read that in the papers, too.

NORRIS: That was a very interesting story about *you* in the papers— something about new evidence. Don't you think it's a little dangerous for you to be running around alone? You ought to have police protection.

MELSA: I—I have police protection.

NORRIS: Well, I don't blame you for ducking them. *(he looks around)* It's very nice up here—quiet, peaceful. You know, I was in prison—you get kind of used to the quiet. After a while you like it very much.

MELSA: *(staring at Norris intently)* I'm very tired and very sleepy.

NORRIS: You look frightened—maybe you'd better have a cigarette. *(he gets up, puts one in her mouth; he keeps talking)* Don't make believe you aren't scared—because you are. I scare most people.

MELSA: *(with a nervous laugh)* No, you don't. I like you.

NORRIS: I don't think you do, Miss Manton.

MELSA: I helped you—I helped your girl friend.

NORRIS: That was very nice of you. You know, I like you. When I was up in the Big House, I used to think what a thrill it would be to kill the people I hated. I hated Lane because he married Sheila and then mistreated her—I hated Belden because Sheila had to go to him to help her against Lane. I love her. I don't look like a lover, do I?

MELSA: You do—very much.

NORRIS: I love Sheila very much. It sounds mixed up, but it's really very clear. I loved Sheila and hated everyone around her. I used to sit in my cell and think about killing all of them, but when I did kill them, they were dead and I had no thrill to look forward to any more. After they were dead, it didn't mean a thing. But you—you know how I came up from downtown and back in ten minutes. *(a gleam is in his eyes, though he still speaks in soft tones)* I've got to kill you and I'm wondering how it

80

will feel to kill someone I like. *(he laughs softly to himself)* You think it's strange?

MELSA: *(her voice quavering)* Yes, it's very strange. *(trying to back away)* I've often felt like killing people I didn't like—but not someone I liked.

NORRIS: You're not going to cry? You know, Lane, he cried like a baby.

> *The telephone bell rings. Both of them look toward it. Then Melsa looks at Norris.*

NORRIS: *(continued)* *(quietly)* I don't think you'd better answer it—I wouldn't like to be disturbed.

MELSA: *(desperately; in hopes of getting to the phone)* If you don't let me answer, my maid will be in here.

> *Norris looks at her narrowly, then nods his head. As she walks across to the telephone, he takes an automatic from his pocket and holds it in his lap. Melsa picks up phone.*

MELSA: *(continued)* Hello... yes, Peter. I'm all right. Well, I just didn't want any more policemen cluttering up my life... no, I'm all right I tell you... please don't come up.

NORRIS: *(quietly)* Maybe you'd better have him up.

MELSA: *(covering the mouthpiece with her hand, looking toward Norris)* No, please, no. He doesn't know anything about you.

NORRIS: *(smiling; gently)* I understand about love.

MELSA: *(into phone)* No, there's nobody up here with me... all right... good night—darling... *(very softly)* and I love you very much. *(she hangs up)*

NORRIS: *(getting to his feet)* Better put your coat on—it's gotten pretty chilly in the street.

MELSA: *(speaking quickly and stalling for time)* The police might be outside. I don't know just from where Peter was calling, but they had a lot of men surrounding him—you might not get out of here. Let's wait a little while—maybe in an hour or so, they'll get tired and go away.

NORRIS: Oh, there aren't any police. I know that. I knew you left them at the club. They almost had me there when I took that shot at you. But I was too smart. I wonder how it would feel to kill that Lieutenant Brent. Maybe after a while I'll try it—*(as though hit by a thought)* You aren't expecting somebody?

MELSA: *(quickly covering up)* Oh no, no—who would come visiting at this time of night? I'm not expecting a soul.

The doorbell buzzes.

NORRIS: *(quietly)* Go open the door. If it's the police, tell them you're going to bed. Leave the door to the foyer wide open.

Melsa crosses, exits. Norris steps behind door so that he can see through the hinge crack and shoot if necessary.

INTERIOR FOYER—NIGHT

Melsa opens door. Peter steps in.

PETER: *(joyously)* Repeat what you said over the telephone?

MELSA: *(sharply)* Please go away—I didn't say anything.

PETER: What about that "I love you very much!" What about...

MELSA: *(interrupting)* Not now—please go away—make it tomorrow—

Norris steps into the foyer.

NORRIS: *(quietly)* Hello, Ames—

PETER: *(severely to Melsa)* A gentleman caller—Melsa, have you been two-timing me? I ought to give you the beating of your life!

NORRIS: *(smiling; gently)* You're very lucky, Ames—she loves you very much—like Sheila used to love me—but you're lucky because you won't ever have to torture yourself thinking about her being married to someone else—when she falls out of love with you. *(the gun appears in his hand)*

PETER: What is this act about?

MELSA: He killed Lane and Belden—He used an electric handcar in the new subway to get there and back.

NORRIS: Suppose we go.

PETER: *(desperately)* She gave you a break with the alibi, didn't she, Norris? I give you my word, we'll do nothing about this till tomorrow. Take a head start and beat it—if they do nab you, I'll play you up sympathetically in the papers, I'll...

VOICE (NORRIS): *(interrrupting; plaintively)* I've got to kill her—and you, too—I've just got to—come on.

Gun pointed, he forces them through door.

82

INTERIOR CORRIDOR—NIGHT

As Norris, gun in pocket, walks behind Melsa and Peter to elevator.

NORRIS: Please don't speak to anyone—I don't want to kill an innocent bystander.

PETER: That's what I like about crazy men—their fine sense of distinction.

NORRIS: *(a crazy gleam enters his eyes)* You think I'm insane?

MELSA: *(quickly, seeing the gleam)* He says that to everybody.

The self-operating elevator appears—they step into it.

INTERIOR ELEVATOR—NIGHT

As Norris presses button and they begin to descend—panel of light indicating their downward trip. Melsa and Peter stand very close together.

PETER: *(with a wry smile)* We've certainly had a short and snappy courtship, haven't we?

Melsa, eyes full, just nods.

PETER: *(continued)* Do you know that little church on Twelfth Street?

Melsa shakes her head in the negative.

PETER: *(continued)* My mother and father were married there—I was baptized there—and when my mother died—*(he stops)*

Melsa slips her hand into his.

PETER: *(continued)* I thought maybe you would have forgotten about a big wedding—we'd have asked a couple of strangers off the street as witnesses—

MELSA: I'd have liked that—

PETER: I knew it—

MELSA: *(whispering)* I'm scared, Peter—I'm scared.

PETER: *(squeezing her hand)* In case I forget—or maybe don't get a chance to tell you—I'm very happy to have loved you!

The elevator stops, the door opens.

INTERIOR LOBBY—NIGHT

As they step from the elevator and begin to cross to the door. The lobby seems deserted. As the three of them get halfway across, Brent and several policemen appear from behind objects. Norris pulls the gun from his pocket.

BRENT: Norris, put that gun down—you'll never get out of here alive.

Norris begins to lift his gun toward Melsa.

NORRIS: First, I'll...

BRENT: *(sharply) Norris—put—that—gun—down!* You're covered from all sides.

Suddenly the girls burst in through the door, getting in the way of the police.

GIRLS: (ad libs) What's up!

We got your phone call!

Are they arresting us again!

Why can't they make their arrests in the daytime.

HELEN: *(seeing Norris's gun)* He's got a gun.

BRENT: *(to girls)* Get out of the way!

NORRIS: Stay where you are.

MELSA: He's going to kill me!

MYRA: If you kill her—you've got to kill all of us.

KIT: You're always talking communism.

Norris starts to lift his gun.

Close shot of Helen as she very quietly bends down, takes a shoe off her foot.

BRENT'S VOICE: *NORRIS—PUT—THAT—GUN—DOWN.*

Full shot. Norris is about to shoot. Helen's shoe comes flying in and hits Norris on the head. The gun goes off. Brent clasps his left shoulder and goes down. The girls pounce on Norris and struggle with him. Peter and police join the melee. Dora runs to Brent and tries to help him up, but Brent pushes her away. Melsa joins the struggling group around Norris.

MELSA: Peter! Peter, darling!

Medium shot. Peter had Norris in front of him and is squaring off to hit him. Some of the girls are holding Norris. Melsa grabs hold of Peter.

MELSA: *(continued)* Peter! Watch, you'll get hurt!

Lee and Kit excitedly try to get Melsa off Peter. Melsa swings in the air and hits Peter. He staggers back into a cluster of girls and the girls go down.

Medium shot. Brent is on the floor. Dora is still trying to help him up. He pushes her away. He has a gun in his other hand. Propping

84

his elbow up on the ground, he aims at Norris. A girl's leg comes into view and the heel of her shoe comes down on Brent's hand. Brent winces.

Full shot. The struggle is still going on. The girls are throwing things—lamps, ashtrays, anything they can find.

Medium shot. Dora has just gotten Brent to his feet. A woman's bag comes flying into scene, hits Dora, who thereupon drops Brent to the floor.

Full shot. Norris emerges from the crowd and makes a dash for the exit.

Close shot—Brent on the ground. He props his arm up, aims at Norris and shoots.

Full shot. Norris, at the steps, crumples to the floor.

HELEN: *(excitedly)* I got him! I got him! I threw the shoe!

The girls, Brent, and Peter reach Norris and bend over him.

HELEN: *(continued) (turning to Brent)* Well, Inspector, again you've got to thank us! *I* threw that shoe!

Brent shakes his left hand at the girls. Suddenly he winces, drops his left hand, and starts to wave his right hand at the girls.

BRENT: *Thank* you! You dumb cluck! I had a gun in my pocket all the time.

PETER: Hilda was listening in on my call—she told me Norris was there. We arranged this!

BRENT: I could have shot him any time I wanted to. I wanted him *alive,* you dopes!

He faints. Melsa and Peter catch him as he goes down.

Close three shot—Melsa, Peter, and Brent, Peter and Melsa leaning over the prone body of Brent, slapping his hands.

PETER AND MELSA: *(ad libs)* Mike, Mike!

Come to.

Don't pass out that way.

Stop being a sissy!

It's Pete talking to you—your old friend, Pete.

Mike!

Melsa's and Peter's heads are quite close together. They look at each other. They can't take their eyes off each other. The slapping of Brent's wrists slows up.

85

PETER: *(in a whisper)* Darling!

MELSA: Darling.

They stop slapping Brent's wrists entirely.

PETER: Let's get married soon.

MELSA: Today.

PETER: I'll get a leave of absence. We'll go to South America—stay there six months. Maybe we won't ever come back.

MELSA: Can you afford it?

PETER: No—but *you* can.

MELSA: *(her eyes narrowing)* I want to live on *your* income.

PETER: That's foolish. Who's going to live on yours?

BRENT: *(opens his eye)* So you're going to marry her after all?

PETER: Yep.

BRENT: Well,—if you want to go through life that way—

Suddenly he hooks his arm around Melsa's neck, draws her down, gives her a violent kiss, lets go of her. Melsa comes up limp. Peter stares at them.

BRENT: *(continued)* *(modestly; examining his fingernails)* Try and top that.

For a moment Peter stares at him.

PETER: Watch this.

His arms go for Melsa. The camera travels down to a giant close shot of Brent's face as his eyes widen and pop at what he sees off scene.

BRENT: *(hoarsely)* SULLIVAN—a bicarbonate of soda!

FADE OUT

THE END